Your Safety and Privacy Online

The CIA and NSA

Siggi Bjarnason

Published by InfoSecHelp LLC, 2019.

While every precaution has been taken in the preparation of this book, the publisher assumes no responsibility for errors or omissions, or for damages resulting from the use of the information contained herein.

YOUR SAFETY AND PRIVACY ONLINE

First edition. September 7, 2019.

Copyright © 2019 Siggi Bjarnason.

ISBN: 978-1-7333068-6-7

Written by Siggi Bjarnason.

Copyediting by Jennifer Schwartz

Proofreading by Catherine Dunn

Cover by Flor Figueroa

COLONFILM
DAVID COLÓN & FLOR FIGUEROA

Library of Congress Control Number:2019910732

Table of Contents

Table of Figures

About This Book

I've been working in the information technology (IT) field for over 30 years now. I recently switched from Network Engineering, a field I've worked in for two decades, into the field of cybersecurity. Cybersecurity is the field of securing computer systems and the information they hold from hostile intrusions.

After some time working in that field, I noticed a severe lack of training for the average computer user on how to be safe online. There is talk in the industry about uneducated end users; meanwhile, all training in that area requires a computer degree to understand. So, in my typical fashion, I decided to do something about this, rather than just simply complaining about it.

After completing a master's degree in Cybersecurity, I set up the website InfoSecHelp, which can be accessed at (https://infosechelp.net/). InfoSec is another term for cybersecurity, focusing on the information rather than the system, but it is essentially the same thing. With this site, I aim to do my part in addressing the information gap.

This book is my first step in this endeavor. I aim to provide all the information an average computer user, without a technical background, would need to stay safe online in a friendly, helpful, and humorous manner. Hopefully, I hit the mark on all fronts and my dry sense of humor doesn't fall flat. Please let me know how you feel I did in achieving my goals.

Any feedback you may have on how to improve this book is greatly appreciated. You can reach me via e-mail at siggi@infosechelp.net. The volume of e-mails I receive will dictate how quickly I can respond. I will try to respond to all e-mails as soon as possible.

The feedback I'm particularly interested in includes but is not limited to:

- What concept or topics do I need to explain more thoroughly? Please be specific.
- Any items I am not covering that you feel the average user needs to know in order to be safe online.
- Does the content flow well? If not, how would you suggest I fix it?
- Are there any spelling, grammar, or formatting mistakes?
- Any general errors or omissions?

BTW all links in this books are also available on our website (https://infosechelp.net/links.php). If you are interested staying in touch and learning what I'm doing next, please sign up for email updates at (https://www.infosechelp.net/subscribe.php) and follow us on twitter @infosechelp.

About the Author

Siggi Bjarnason is an expert cybersecurity professional with four decades of computer and online experience. Born in Iceland, Siggi spent much of his adult life in Seattle, Washington. In Washington, he lived through the development of a groundbreaking form of technology that would revolutionize not only the tech industry but the world as we know it. Everyone now knows this groundbreaking technology as the internet.

In the early 1980s, while still a teenager, Siggi developed an interest in computers as a hobby. By the mid-1990s, he turned that hobby into a profession. You could say that he was a pioneer in the birth of the internet when he worked as a network engineer at Microsoft during its infancy. Siggi has communicated and explored online since the mid-1980s, even though the first public web browser wasn't available until 1994.

Siggi's newest venture, InfoSecHelp, is specifically designed to help those with limited technical knowhow to stay safe online. It doesn't matter if it is a home computer, small business, or large enterprise, InfoSecHelp can help.

Siggi's enthusiasm for technology is what drives him to find new ways to help people stay on top of the changing digital landscape. By assisting people in remaining safe online and avoiding scams that could damage their systems and their wallets, he hopes computer users can fully enjoy the marvels of the internet.

In his free time, Siggi enjoys the simple things in life like listening to music, attending live theater events, and going ballroom dancing. Additionally, Siggi enjoys volunteering for organizations that help his community. He is a volunteer for the American Red Cross, Public Health Reserve Corps (PHRC), and other similar organizations. For Siggi, nothing is more important than finding ways to enjoy life, whether that be through computers, working with others, or listening to his favorite album.

Introduction

The purpose of this book is to provide the average computer user with the knowledge that will help them stay safe while online. Additionally, it will help them make the privacy choices that work for them. My goal is to explain online threats in terms that don't require a technical background to understand. All technical jargon will be limited, and when necessary, it will first be explained in standard nontechnical terms.

This book should be accessible to anyone with enough computer knowledge to use Facebook, Twitter, and other social media. Some other activities include online shopping, using Google to search for cat videos, and even paying your bills online. If you are comfortable doing those things, then you are in the core demographic for this book.

I wrote this book with a US consumer in mind, but this book is equally applicable for people all over the world. There may be an occasional inside joke that people outside the USA might not understand, but that shouldn't detract from the learning process.

What is different about this book is that I'm targeting nontechnical users. I explain the issues and the threats without resorting to the scare tactics or threats which seem so prevalent in today's security training. Fear, Uncertainty, and Doubt (FUD), is very commonplace in today's information security space. I avoid all FUD in this book.

If I were to summarize this book in a few short points, it would be:

- Don't click on links or attachments in unexpected e-mails.
- Never share your password. Use a password manager for all your passwords.
- Use long, unpredictable, and unique passwords for every site.
- Use critical thinking skills.
- Finally, when an e-mail, text message, phone call, or online article riles up your emotions, then you are more likely to fall for a scam.

In addition to pointing out and explaining online threats, I will also help you understand what to do about them. I will avoid being prescriptive; instead, I will focus on helping you make your own decisions. To accomplish this, I may give you more ideas to consider and even suggest some research for you, the reader, to do on your own, rather than feeding you all the answers. When appropriate, I may lay out a few options and outline the pros and cons of each option so that you can make the choice that is right for you.

There are a few inherently dangerous things, and I will strongly advise you against them. This may include saying, "Do not do this under any circumstances." While that may sound like a command, it is intended as recommended advice. I will explain my reasons for any advice offered. Areas where this type of advice comes up is very rare in this book.

The focus of this book, as the title implies, is online safety. I draw on analogies from the physical world, use examples from physical security, and even address other ideas regarding your physical security. Physical security is outside the scope of this book. The reason I relate things to physical security and use examples from that area is because most people can relate to physical security more easily than to online security.

Since I'm writing this book for nontechnical users, I try to avoid thinking, "I don't need to say X; everyone knows that." For that reason, certain sections or chapters may seem obvious and self-explanatory. Just know that this is intentional and that you have a little more knowledge than the target audience. So if you come across something you already know, then you are ahead of the pack, and I hope you will still get valuable knowledge out of this book.

General Principles

I will begin by going over some general principles. I will give you some foundation to leverage as you start on your online security journey.

Threat Modeling

The first thing I need to discuss is the concept of threat modeling. Threat modeling is the action of deliberately thinking through and cataloging potential threats in your everyday life. Threat Landscape is another term used in this context. These terms come from the idea that you can create a model or a landscape picture of all the things that pose a threat to you. This picture illustrates the concept of a threat:

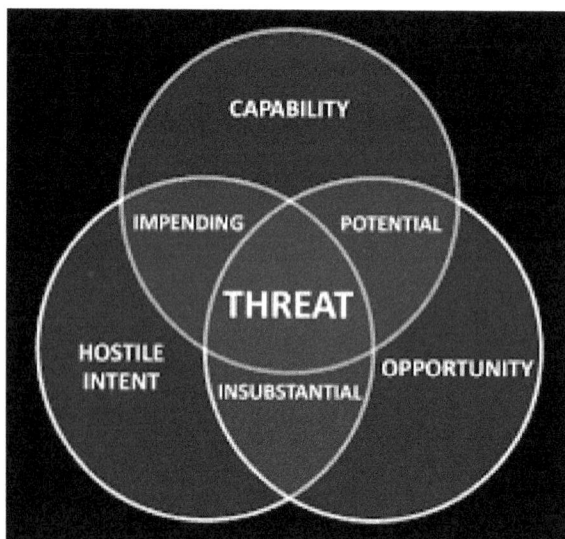

Figure 1: Definition of a threat

Let's discuss this picture and explore the lessons it holds. At a high level, it is saying that for something to be a threat, you need to have three ingredients. Any avid crime mystery readers or those who like to watch crime shows on television will recognize these ingredients. These ingredients are intent, opportunity, and capability. Crime shows on television often label intent as motive. Without the three elements present at the same time, then you have no real threat.

The term *capability* refers to having the ability to do something. This ingredient is present in most of the cases involving threats to our physical wellbeing. Most of us possess the physical ability to do unspeakable harm to another living creature. Luckily, most of us are decent human beings who could never even imagine harming another person.

In other words, we lack the hostile intent to do harm to others. Going back to capability, when it comes to online threats, this element is frequently missing, as it requires a good deal of technical knowledge for someone to be a menace online. So those without technical knowledge lack the capability to be a threat online. Regardless of how much they desire to be a menace, they can never become a real threat online until they gain the required technical skills.

Opportunity is the concept of having access to something. It's about being in the right place at the right time and with access to the target. In the physical world, this means having access to the person you wish to harm. Personal bodyguards and diplomatic protection details rely heavily on removing opportunity from the equation in order to keep the person they are protecting safe from harm. They can't control a person's intent, nor can they control a person's capabilities; however, they can manage opportunities. As we discussed, there is no threat without all three components. By controlling public access to the person they are protecting, they limit the opportunity factor, thus limiting the threat and the risk.

The last element is the concept of *intent*, sometimes called motive or desire. If people have no ill will towards you and do not wish you harm, they pose no real threat to you. Returning to physical protection methods, including bodyguards, the concept of security screening deals in this space. Security screening tries to assess if you hold any ill will towards those who are under security protection.

This can be difficult to determine and can change without any notice or warning. We see this when an originally peaceful place suddenly becomes a hotspot of violence. In most cases, the folks involved didn't suddenly gain new opportunities or obtain new capabilities. Most of the time, something happens to trigger the mass of people to gain a newfound desire and motivation to take things into their own hands.

As you see in the Venn diagram, the following situation occurs when one of the elements is missing:

Opportunity + Capability = Potential Threat
Opportunity + Hostile Intent = Insubstantial Threat

Hostile Intent + Capability = Impending Threat
All Three = Actual Threat

As you may have observed, this is a very fluid concept; all three concepts can change without notice and change the risk level in an instant. You may only have a potential threat because the intent is missing; then something happens and a friend becomes a foe, and now there is intent. Someone may not have the capability, then they learn a new skill and now they have the capability. There may not be an opportunity one moment, then the next moment an opportunity arises.

Then there is the concept of *vulnerability*. In the physical realm, we are all vulnerable to physical attacks, including someone shooting, stabbing, or beating us. Some people are more vulnerable than others, depending on their self-defense capabilities. I think it is safe to say that all humans are vulnerable to gunshots regardless of their training. Protective gear, such as helmets and bulletproof vests, can reduce that vulnerability. Additionally, faulty protective gear, such as a bulletproof vest that doesn't stop bullets, gives you a false sense of security and leaves you vulnerable.

Now apply this idea to your online world; depending on your training, condition, and protective gear, your vulnerability online varies. The goal of this book is to provide training and introduce you to the necessary protective gear so that you can reduce your online vulnerabilities.

The last major concept when it comes to threat modeling is the concept of *risk*. Risk is mathematically expressed as the multiplication of threat and vulnerability. In other words, your risk factor becomes higher as your vulnerability and threats increase. If both factors are high, your risk is significantly higher. I'm very mathematically inclined, but I know that not everyone is, so let me lay out some basic multiplications to illustrate this:

- $1 \times 1 = 1$
- $1 \times 5 = 5$
- $1 \times 10 = 10$
- $5 \times 1 = 5$
- $5 \times 5 = 25$
- $10 \times 1 = 10$
- $10 \times 10 = 100$

The lower your risk —the number after the equals sign—the less chance you have of becoming a victim. There is no such thing as zero threats or zero vulnerabilities, and thus, there is no such thing as zero risk. In other words, you can have an exceptionally low risk, but you will never be completely without risk.

Because the concept of a threat is fluid, your threat model will be equally fluid and requires frequent re-evaluation. So now, back to the idea of a threat model, also called threat landscape or threat analysis. Just a footnote: in the world of threat intelligence, these words have a slightly different meaning; however, for our purposes, they are the same.

So how does one create this threat model? All you do is think of all the things that pose a threat to you.

You don't have to justify the threats to anyone; this can be based on a gut feeling, intuition, or experience. You may want to keep this to yourself and not share it with anyone or you may decide to share it. If you do share it with someone and they call you paranoid, that can be a good thing as it indicates you've taken a potential threat seriously. This will be a very individual and personal model and one that can be influenced by many factors. It is an informal thing you do for yourself; whether you write it down or keep it in your head is up to you.

For an example of how threat models change from person to person, consider this. In general, women will have a completely different threat model from men. For women, hundreds of everyday tasks, from getting gas to buying groceries, include a wide range of threats to their wellbeing. Typically, men don't have to worry about those things.

Here is another example of how a threat model can differ from one person to another. Think about a dissident living in China, Russia, or any other country where the government doesn't like to be questioned. This person will have a complex threat model. In contrast, let's think about a person who lives in a country where free speech is protected. This person may have an ordinary, dull job and they aren't involved in anything but a bowling league. Their threat model is straightforward in comparison and starkly different.

- Here are some other ideas on the concept of threat models and how they can vary significantly from person to person. For a large section of the population, the chance of a random person roofieing them at a bar is a real threat to their safety. Some might say this could affect as many as 40–50 percent of the population.

- Some people are concerned with being hacked by a random hacker, especially if they are attending a conference that is popular with hackers.
- Some people truly and honestly believe that anyone using any product made in China, whether it is software or electronics, is certifiably insane.

None of these people are wrong; it is all a matter of perspective, personal situation, and background. Based on what I have read, out of the threats listed above, being roofied is the most significant danger to the largest population. All of those scenarios are real threats to different people. This shows that threat profiling is very personal and varied. The big thing to keep in mind is that just because something isn't a threat to you, doesn't mean it doesn't pose a threat to someone else and vice versa.

Speaking of China, there is a lot of news lately regarding a company called Huawei and the Chinese government allegedly spying on people. Let's use the Venn diagram above to analyze some of that news.

- Is the Chinese government capable of spying on anyone they wish? Absolutely. I do not doubt their capability in that area.

- Do they have the opportunity to spy on anyone they want? There is a high probability that they do. Those who believe that anyone who uses Chinese products is insane would certainly argue that they do. For the record, I believe they have a very compelling argument. I would even say that if the Chinese government wanted to spy on you, they could do so even if you only use products made in the US.

- Do they have the intent to spy on everyone in the world? This is unlikely. Is the Chinese government spying on billions of people, especially Chinese citizens and others who oppose them? Absolutely; there is no doubt about it. Are they spying on some US citizens? This is highly likely.

Who you are, where you've been, where you are from, and what you do are all factors that influence your threat model. Just because you aren't concerned about something and the person right next to you is, that doesn't make either of you wrong. Debating about how someone should be concerned about something that you are concerned about but they aren't is as valid as discussing how someone should love peanut butter just because you love peanut butter. For the record, I hate even the smell of peanut butter, and this makes me an odd person in the US.

As with all personal matters, you can talk about why you are or why you are not concerned about something, but shaming someone for having a different take on things is never alright. Any form of shaming is never acceptable.

For you to be effective in your quest to be more security conscious, you need to take the time and really think through your threat model. Think about all the things that could threaten your daily life, and make sure you dig deeper. This should encompass both physical threats and online threats. As you work through this, make sure you include counter-measures, as in how to respond to those threats. Start with physical threats and then add online threats as you progress through this book.

Start with the big things, for example, is there anything in your daily routine that threatens your life? Do you live in an area with high murder or assault rates? If so, what precautions do you usually take, and how do you deal with that threat? From there, you can branch out into the other things that pose a threat to your way of life. Don't limit this to things that could end your life; that is just a starting point. Include things that could significantly impact your quality of life.

This should be detailed and not on a high level. Think about who and what could threaten your way of life. For example, getting laid off from work might be on the threat model for many people; however, you need to go deeper than that. What are some situations that might lead to you being laid off?

Losing your life savings or becoming a victim of an assault or mugging are other possibilities for the physical threat model. For every possibility, go deeper than just one or two words. These are examples from the physical world that I imagine most people can identify with.

After reading this book, you will be able to integrate online activities into your threat model as well. A good threat model covers all aspects of your everyday life. It is also iterative and always evolving, as I identified above. As I mentioned, a threat model is a highly individual and personal thing that you can do to help you gain an understanding of any threats in your life. You should never have to justify it, and who you share it with is up to you. It is normal and acceptable not to share your threat model with anyone.

Threat Actors

Let us touch on the concept of a *threat actor*. A threat actor is simply the person or people perpetrating the threat. Threat actor is a synonym for criminal, and I use these terms interchangeably. It can refer to a single person but is more often a group of people, such as organized crime families, also known as the mafia. While in the past the mob has focused on physical crime, they joined the online crime game several years ago. Here are some common threat actor types.

Nation-State Threat Actors

Nation-state threat actors are criminal organizations sponsored by a country. Russia, China, North Korea, and others are considered to have nation-state threat actors. There are some people who even say that the United States National Security Agency and the Central Intelligence Agency are nation-state threat actors.

Advanced Persistent Threats (APTs)

APTs are highly sophisticated threat actor groups that have significant resources at their disposal. Once they select a target, they will not stop until they've accomplished their mission. These groups tend to be funded by a nation-state or another organization with deep pockets.

Both APT and nation-state groups typically have a particular task that their sponsors gain specific benefits from, often in terms of reputation, revenge, or information. If an APT group targets you, there really isn't much you can do beyond moving in with the Amish to stop them. Most APT groups appear not to be financially motivated, but North Korea is a notable exception.

Organized Crime Groups

As previously mentioned, these are classic mafia groups turned high tech. Their motive tends to be simple—money—and their motive mirrors their tactics in the physical world. Their missions are all about direct financial gain or gaining something that they can easily monetize.

Hacktivists

In the physical world, these are usually called eco-terrorists. They claim that they are operating for a higher cause. They tend to attack companies and people they feel they need to teach a lesson. They believe that they can teach them the necessary lesson by hacking them, breaking into their system, stealing from them, defacing their websites with their message, or through other methods.

Random Threat Actor

These are individual threat actors that are in it for a myriad of reasons. Some are in it merely for the financial gain, while others are just trying to settle a grudge. A random threat actor could be a disgruntled employee, an unhappy customer, or even just a friend turned foe because they felt slighted.

Script Kiddies

As the name implies, these are often teenagers or young adults doing irresponsible things just because they can. Often they have no real mission. Some are just seeking excitement and seeing what they can do—typical teenage stuff—while others are attempting to make some easy money. There is a lot of crossover between script kiddies and random threat actors. The random threat actor is usually more sophisticated than a script kiddy, and they often have more technical knowledge.

Privacy

Privacy can have a very direct impact on your security. Whether we are talking about physical or virtual privacy, the extent of the impact will vary depending on your threat model. For example, if you have an abusive stocker in your life, having them know where you live might impact your security and your life. So, in that scenario, keeping your address private is critical to your physical security.

Some preach that privacy is one size fits all, that it is critical that everyone become private for the sake of their own security. They have a very prescriptive approach to privacy. I do not agree with this message, and I equate them with those who believe that everyone should dress conservatively and never show any skin. While that may work for some people, it does not work for everyone.

We are all different; we have different opinions and different approaches to living. Those differences are just that—differences; no method is plainly right or wrong. They, in a way, make us who we are. I believe in helping people understand how to adopt safe online practices in their way of life.

How can you be aware of your privacy and operate safely online – what is often referred to as operational security – without drastically changing who you are or how you act? You shouldn't have to adapt your life to some fixed set of rules, because, like I said, there is more than one right way of doing things. You should be able to adapt the rules that work best for your life.

To accomplish that, you need to think about your privacy stance. This usually factors heavily into your threat model; one might say that your privacy stance reflects your threat model. For example, is it a problem for you if your address or phone number is publicly known? Your address, phone numbers, e-mails, and social security numbers are referred to as Personally Identifiable Information (or PII).

PII is any piece of information or combination of information that can uniquely identify you. A general best practice is to limit the distribution of your PII. If you have considered the implications and you have a case that works for you for advertising your PII to everyone, that is your decision to make. Just be mindful about your approach to privacy. Also, keep in mind that once it is publicly available, you can't take it back.

So, in short, your privacy stance is about being very mindful about what you post online and thinking through how that would impact your threat model.

Physical Address Privacy

If you need the general public to have an address where they can send you mail while keeping your residential address private, then a private mailbox is the perfect solution. Typically, this is a storefront in a local strip mall that manages packing and shipping. As an added service they offer apartment-style mailboxes that they rent out.

What you end up with is an address that looks like a regular street address because it is the address of the store plus your box number. These stores typically don't care how your mail arrives—USPS, FedEx, UPS, DHL, or Messenger—as long as it is marked with your name and box number. Shop around for the location that is most convenient for you and that offers the services and prices that work for you. Some offer notification services; others charge a fee for handling anything other than letters. Those handling fees are usually on top of your monthly rental costs. If you regularly shop online, this can add up quickly.

Some only handle letters and won't handle packages. So be sure to inquire about the service offerings, limits, and any additional charges. MailBoxes Etc.,

Pony Express, and the UPS store are some of the chain stores available, but there are plenty of others out there, so shop around. I recommend staying away from PO boxes at the post office, as you can only receive mail there if it was sent via the US Postal Service, plus you get the level of customer service the US Postal Service is known for.

In addition to offering privacy, these services also improve the physical security of your physical mail. To my knowledge, there has never been a case of mail theft via those facilities.

One service deserves special mention here, as it can do wonders for privacy and security in real life and online. This service is called Traveling Mailbox:

(https://travelingmailbox.com/?ref=540). This is a service I just discovered in early July 2019, as I was finishing up this book, but it shows great promise. Initial testing seems to indicate a few days' lag between them receiving something for you and you seeing it, but the data is still inconclusive.

They offer a similar service to the UPS Store and Pony Express; however, unlike those stores where you must show up in person, with Traveling Mailbox everything is online. It's like a bridge between your online and your physical world. They will accept your physical mail, scan it, and then e-mail you the image.

For those who don't know what a scan is, it is like taking a photo of a piece of paper with your computer. Then, once you've reviewed the scan of the letter or other mail, you can instruct them to shred it or forward it to wherever you are in the world at that time. You can also upload a document you have on your computer and they will print it and mail it out for you.

Where this can be helpful in the physical world is when surveillance is part of your threat model. When using the UPS Store, for example, a criminal isn't going to know the address you reside at. However, they could surveil the location that receives your mail and wait for you to show up to collect it. With the Traveling Mailbox, you never show up at your address, which takes the surveillance option off the table.

Now, as I've said before, there is no perfect security solution. The best you can do is make things difficult for the threat actors in your threat model—maybe shift things around a little. While using services such as Traveling Mailbox may limit your surveillance concerns, it doesn't eliminate them. Also, if your threat actor is persistent, they'll find a different way to track you down, such as breaking into the Traveling Mailbox systems.

Now, as you may have guessed by their name, they are targeting their service towards people who travel a lot, allowing them to easily receive their mail while on the road.

For complete transparency, I want to disclose that if you use the link above with ref=540, it will let them know that I referred you and they will give me a few dollars. If you are uncomfortable with this, feel free to leave it off the URL. My goal is not to sell you any service or product but to make you aware of the options out there that I feel might be well suited to certain situations. Always research everything and never take anything at face value. Decide for yourself what works best for your situation.

Once Posted, It Never Goes Away

One thing that is crucial to keep in mind when it comes to privacy is that when you post something online, it will never go away. So when you are tweeting, posting on Facebook, or using Instagram or Tumblr, think about how this will look 10–20 years from now. Even if you try to delete something, you never know who has saved it or forwarded it somewhere else. You don't even know for sure whether the site deleted your post or just hid it.

Even with a service like Snapchat, I know many people who screenshot every message. A screenshot is when you take a picture of your screen. Also, what assurance do we have that Snapchat isn't keeping an archive? Have you heard of the Wayback Machine (https://archive.org/web/)? If not, check it out and be ready to have your mind blown. The point being: write and post as if you are writing on a permanent public record that you can never erase. And again, be mindful about how what you post impacts your threat model.

Loading Remote Content in E-mails

All modern e-mail clients offer a privacy feature that is often overlooked or misunderstood. This is the option not to load remote images and other remote content. When you allow loading of remote photos or content, the sender will not only know exactly when you opened their message but also generally where you opened it from. When you turn this off, it will only impact marketing e-mails, spam, and scam e-mails, and it will make them look all weird and bland. In return, the marketer doesn't know when you read their mail or where you read it. In some cases, it has been known to download viruses to the computer it is viewed on when you automatically download remote content.

By turning off automatic loading of remote content, you are trading attractive ads for privacy. You still have the option of loading remote content on an e-mail by e-mail basis. Below are some screenshots from popular e-mail clients with this setting. Please note, I was not able to get this to work reliably with my Outlook (aka Hotmail) account; this setting seems to always be on (allowed). I found a setting that appeared turned on by default, and I turned it off. Even after I turned it off, remote content still loaded.

ProtonMail

ProtonMail, a privacy-centric e-mail service based in Switzerland, allows you to adjust this privacy setting. This photo below shows how you can turn off loading of remote content. These are the default settings shown below.

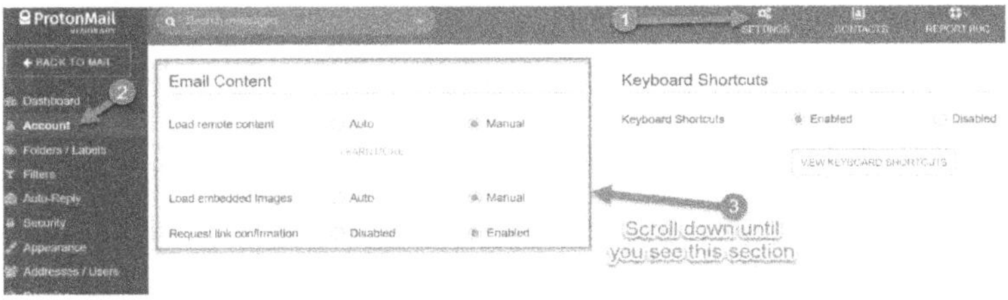

Figure 2: ProtonMail e-mail content settings

In their client, here is how to load remote content manually on an e-mail by e-mail basis.

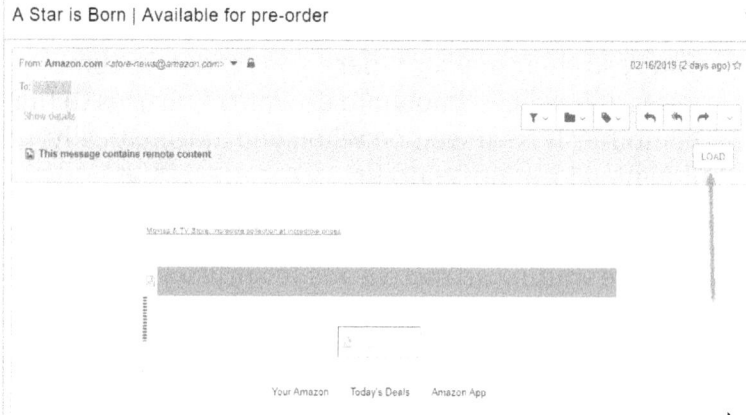

Figure 3: Promotional e-mail in ProtonMail

I highly recommend and fully endorse ProtonMail as an e-mail service. I subscribe at their visionary level, and I've been using this service since March 2018. I receive no benefits for recommending them.

Thunderbird Mail

The location of the option to turn off loading of remote content in Thunderbird's e-mail service is shown below.

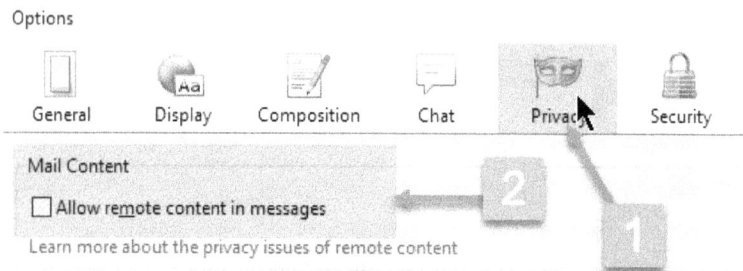

Figure 4: Thunderbird settings

Figure 5: Example promotional e-mail - option off

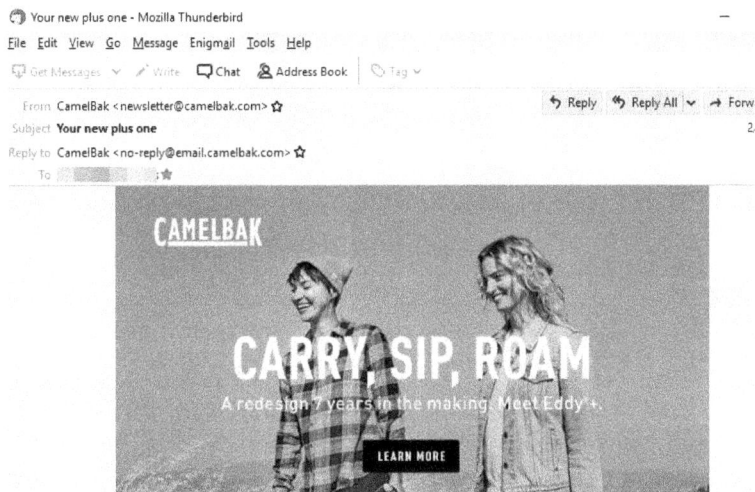

Figure 6: Truncated example remote content loaded

Gmail

Here is this privacy setting in Gmail; you need to scroll down to find this.

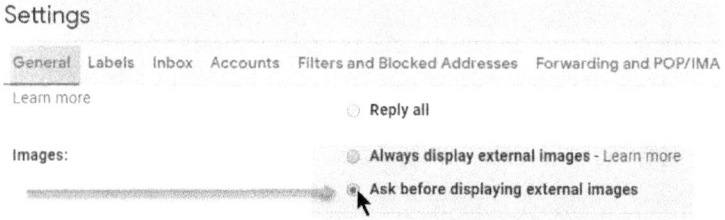

Figure 7: Gmail setting

Figure 8: The same e-mail - option turned off in Gmail

Outlook Application

Microsoft seems to have buried this setting deep within the Outlook application, so it took me some time to find it. On the plus side, it is detailed and works well. Below is a step-by-step pictorial on how to find it.

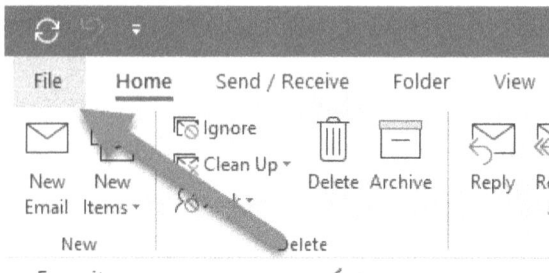

Figure 9: Outlook Step 1

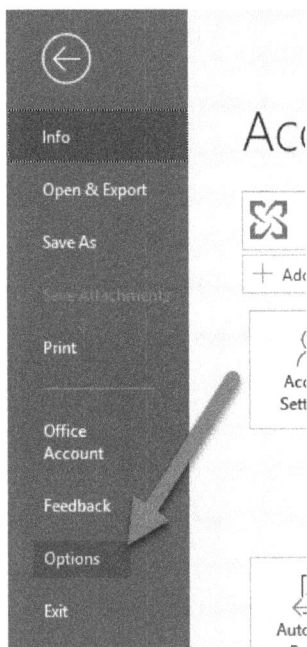

Figure 10: Outlook Step 2

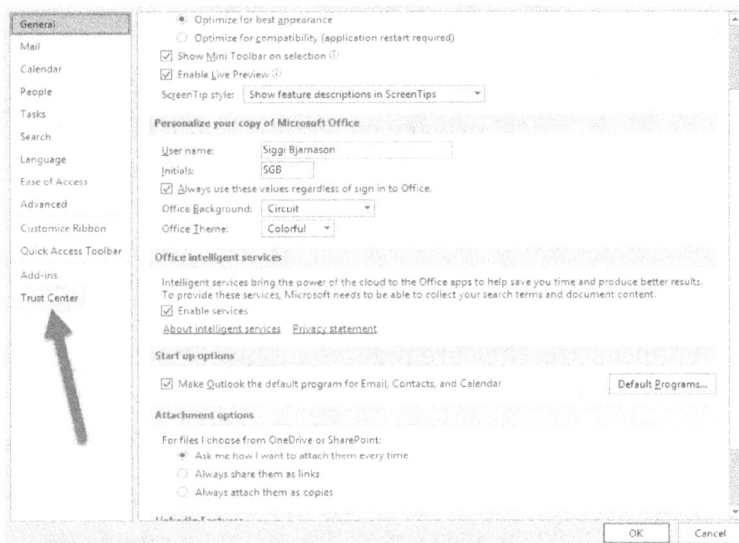

Figure 11:Outlook Step 3

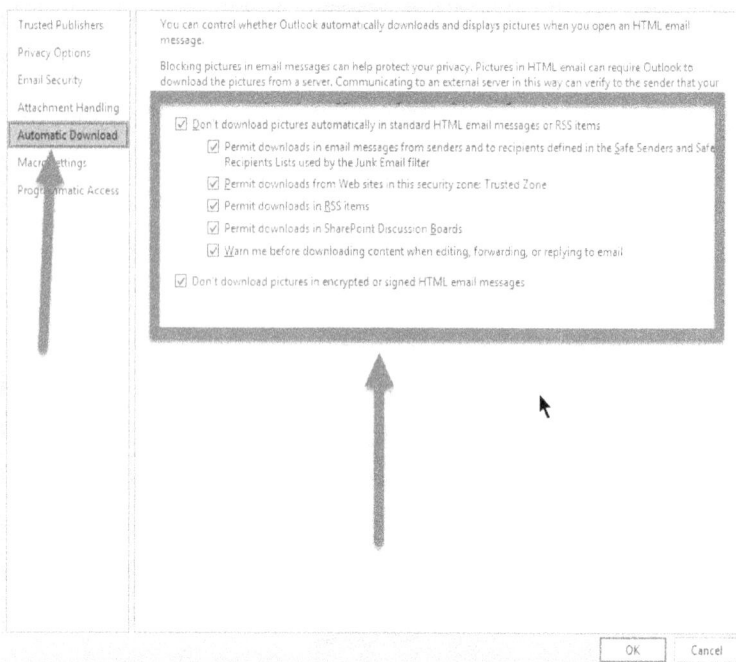

Figure 12: Outlook Step 4: The final step

Free Stuff

Another critical privacy concept is that if you're not a paying customer, you're the product. What this is speaking to is the idea that most companies like to make money, or at least break even. If you're not paying them, how are they making their money or paying for the cost of providing their service to you? Chances are, they are making money by selling your information to other companies. Here is a thought exercise for you. Is that cool game free because the game creator is benevolent and has given the product away for free for the betterment of humankind? Or are they trying to make money?

Granted, every now and then someone creates something in their spare time just for fun and to see if they can succeed. This is a tiny fraction of everything out there, and this kind of product usually comes with no support, updates, or fixes. Using a product that isn't supported can be a bad security problem. I'll get into the why later, in the section on keeping your computer updated.

The notable exception to this is the open-source community. The open-source community releases free software with no strings attached, just to be helpful, and the members keep it updated as well. They are typically run on donations only and are not for profit. The developers donate their time to make and maintain the software, and donations pay for hosting fees and other operational costs. You need to carefully assess if the product is truly open-source, and if it truly is an open-source product then what are their operating and financial models?

Now we come to the question of what is the business of the business? Or how does a company make the bulk of its income? A prime example is that McDonald's is in the real estate business, not in the restaurant business. This is because the McDonald's Corporation owns a lot of real estate and land, and therefore it gets the bulk of its revenue from renting buildings and land. Hamburger restaurants are just a means to make rent. There is a link to an article titled "What business is McDonald's really in?" in the appendix for further reading on this.

Here is some homework for you. Research what business Google is in and what their main revenue streams are. Google is now a subsidiary of a conglomerate named Alphabet. That does not change the fact that Google must produce a profit. Does Google's profit come from selling a product, selling advertising, or selling users' data?

I'll leave it up to the reader to research the answers to these questions. Also do similar research on Facebook, Twitter, and any other company you are getting a free service from. For publicly traded companies, SEC filings contain a lot of great information. Often just reading the company's website will give you a clue. If a company is known to be profitable, yet there is nothing on their website about selling a product, it makes one wonder where the money is coming from. Here is a tweet from ProtonMail where they are discussing an article from the Business Insider website on this topic: (https://twitter.com/ProtonMail/status/10982372 40726208512?s=03)

> **ProtonMail** ✓
> @ProtonMail
>
> Google did not disclose that its home security system, Nest Secure, contained microphones. businessinsider.com/nest-microphon... Until Google gives up its surveillance economy business model, every Google device is potential spyware. ProtonMail puts user privacy (not advertising) first.

Figure 13: ProtonMail tweet slamming Google

Since Gmail from Google is a direct competitor to ProtonMail, this tweet smells a little like rival trash-talk. Your task is to research all of these claims and find sources unrelated to ProtonMail or the Business

Insider website that either confirm or refute the claims they make. Then you need to come to your own conclusion on the topic.

When a company has a significant revenue stream from advertisements, it is a good idea to scrutinize their privacy policies. It is important to think about how their business model jives with your privacy stance and your threat model. Also, think about whether their privacy policy jives with the company business model and philosophy. Targeted advertisements are not compatible with strict privacy. Remember that it is not possible to create targeted ads without learning details about the targets.

The concept of a targeted ad is considered to be a euphemism for ads you are more likely to believe and fall for. For those who have privacy concerns, it is better to go with a company that bases its revenue on subscriptions, even if it means having to purchase a subscription. It all comes down to what your privacy is worth to you.

Those who are concerned about privacy often buy subscriptions from companies in Switzerland due to the strong privacy laws in that country. The point here is that nothing is free; some products you pay for by giving up your privacy. If that seems like a fair trade-off to you, then there are zero problems as long as you fully understand that there is a trade-off and what you are trading.

Free Seminars

Before I leave the topic of privacy, let's talk about the free seminars you are bound to come across from time to time. I'm not talking about free videos posted on YouTube or papers posted on websites to download for free. What I'm talking about here is when you get e-mails stating "Sign up here to get free training in XYZ," "Sign up for a free webinar on ABC," or "For a free book, sign up here."

There is a reason why they want you to register to download something or to watch something rather than posting the video on YouTube or allowing you to download it directly. That reason is that they can make money with the information you provide during registration. Most companies will even disclose this in the fine print of the registration. It appears in small print because they don't want it to be too obvious, as that might discourage you.

The fine print may say something like:

> *By submitting your registration, you authorize us to release this information to third party partners to promote their products. You explicitly permit them to call you to try to sell you their products.*

In other words, in exchange for letting you watch a sales presentation, you allow them to harass you with sales calls.

Most of these free training resources and webinars that require registration—the ones I've seen, anyway—are just sales presentations disguised as training. That is not to say that you can't learn a lot from sales presentations; they tend to be more high level than technical presentations. The point here is not to talk down free webinars, it is to have you think about the value exchange and be aware that free webinars have a privacy cost to them. In short, the saying that there is no such thing as a free lunch has a lot of truth to it. Even if you aren't paying directly, that doesn't mean it is free.

This is not just about webinars or free training; it applies to anything where you are asked to provide registration details to get something that is listed for free.

Raffles and Drawings

Another example of when you pay for free things with your privacy is by participating in raffles and drawings. If you sign up for a raffle or a free drawing, whether it is online or at an event, how much of your privacy are you giving up? There is a difference between a door prize where they hand you a ticket when you enter a room and when they hand you a registration form for you to enter a drawing. Are they doing the drawing because they want to be kind and give back to the audience, or are they collecting personal information to make money? What about those booths at the mall encouraging you to fill out a form for a chance to win a big prize? Is the prize even real? Something worth thinking about before you submit that raffle entry.

Critical Thinking Skills

Maybe I'm just a curmudgeonly old guy. You know the type—the old man who sits on his front porch in a rocking chair yelling at kids to get off his lawn and talking about the good old days. However, I feel like critical thinking skills are diminishing in our society these days. Hopefully I'm wrong in that sentiment. Critical thinking skills play a pivotal role in your online safety, as you may have noticed already. Whenever and whatever you are doing online, always approach things with a critical mindset. I will go into a little more detail in the next section, but never take anything you read online at face value.

Always approach everything with a skeptical mindset and do your own research. There was a tweet on April Fool's Day that I loved but failed to bookmark so I can't directly quote it or correctly credit it. This tweet said something like, "Welcome to April 1st, the one day a year where people think critically about what they read online." I think there is a lot of truth to this. The message here is that when you are online, the trickery of April Fool's Day happens every day of the year, not just on April 1st. When you are online, behave like it's April Fool's Day and apply that level of scrutiny to everything you see, and don't let the online trolls make a fool of you any day of the year.

I have found that anything with an emotionally charged subject or title is likely to be thin on facts and heavy on emotional manipulation. Typical headlines, subjects, and titles to watch out for include, "You won't believe what X did!" or "Did you see what X did?"

You are going to see a reoccurring theme through this book about questioning everything. Examine everything you read and analyze it using your critical thinking skills. Always ask yourself: does this make sense? Are there ulterior motives?

Paranoia minus Tinfoil Hats

There is a lot of stigma around paranoia, jokes about tinfoil hats, and sayings such as "Just because you are paranoid does not mean they are not out to get you." There is even outright shaming and bullying. There is clinical paranoia and then there is the label placed on those who highly prioritize security and privacy.

Discussion of how harmful shaming and bullying can be, especially when it comes to clinical mental health issues, is far outside the scope of any computer security topic. Suffice it to say, shaming and bullying is always wrong and harmful. The reason I bring it up is that in order to be safe and secure online, you need to risk people calling you paranoid. If you get called or labeled paranoid, take it as a sign that you are probably conducting yourself safely and securely.

I think being a trusting individual is a beautiful quality, I really do. The problem with being too trusting is that people will take advantage of you, you are more prone to fall for scams, and you will be cheated more often. Some people make a conscious choice to remain trusting despite being burned numerous times, and I applaud those people. The problems with being trusting magnify when you go online. To be safe and secure online, you cannot trust anything; you must question everything, and I mean absolutely everything.

When I advise you to trust nothing and question everything, I'm not saying that you can't trust your best friend when you are online, even though you trust them fully in the real world. What I'm saying is: don't trust that you are talking with your best friend; question whether that really is your best friend.

If a person walked up to you in real life who resembled your best friend, and they even sounded kind of like them, but something wasn't right, would you just trust that this really was your best friend or would you be skeptical? Maybe throw them a curveball question to see if they respond like you would expect your friend to answer. This may be a far-fetched example; however, this happens every day online and is easy to pull off.

Questioning everything online will lead to independent critical thinking, which is a beautiful thing. Thinking for yourself and utilizing some critical thinking skills will help you stay safe. Just accepting everything someone tells you without any analysis will only lead to trouble. For example, you get an e-mail that has your friend's name in the "From" field and the body just says something like, "You've got to check this out," and it includes a web link or an attachment. Here is an image of an e-mail like that.

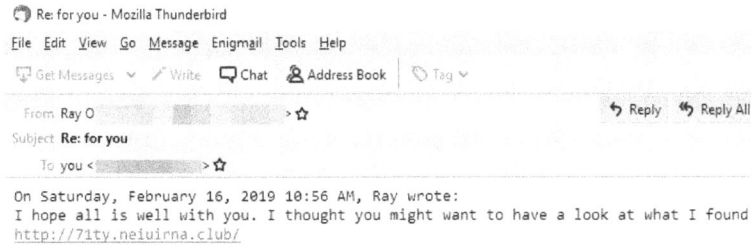

```
Re: for you - Mozilla Thunderbird
File  Edit  View  Go  Message  Enigmail  Tools  Help
  Get Messages  v    Write    Chat    Address Book    Tag  v
  From  Ray O                          >                                    Reply    Reply All
Subject  Re: for you
     To  you <                  >
On Saturday, February 16, 2019 10:56 AM, Ray wrote:
I hope all is well with you. I thought you might want to have a look at what I found
http://71ty.neiuirna.club/
```

Figure 14: Sample spoofed e-mail

In this specific example, I do know Ray, and the e-mail address I blurred out is Ray's e-mail. Our e-mail exchanges have a certain rhythm to them, like I'm sure everyone's does. The first thing that struck me is that this e-mail does not sound like something that I would expect from Ray. It would be out of character for him to send me something like this. So I immediately determined that this was spam. I figured that if I clicked on that link, I would get a virus or malware for my efforts, so instead I just flagged the message as spam and deleted it. If you receive an e-mail like this and you think it might be authentic but you have doubts, this is what I recommend.

Before you click on that link, call your friend or send them a text asking them to explain what that link is all about. If they reply "What link?" then you know it is a malicious link, and you know not to click on it. If they tell you it is this hilarious cat video or some other explanation, you know that it really did come from your friend. However, you don't know if it is safe. This is where critical thinking comes in again.

Is the reward of watching yet another hilarious cat video worth the risk of it being malicious? What is the likelihood that your friend found this video by visiting an unsavory site? I'll cover this in more detail in later sections on malware. The point I want to make here is to be critical of what you read online and don't take things at face value. Also, don't click on links or open attachments that you don't know anything about. One of the most common ways to become a computer security victim is by clicking on a link or by opening an attachment to see what it is.

If you don't know what it is, don't touch it. For example, you are out walking in the downtown area of a major city and you notice a weird substance that you can't visually identify. Street smart people just ignore it and move on, and they don't try to analyze it. A scientist might take out their lab gloves and a specimen tube and get a sample to take back to their lab for analysis. I believe everyone would agree that touching it with your bare hands to analyze this unknown substance is not wise. Same thing here; unless you have the right equipment and the protective gear to analyze those unknown links and attachments scientifically, don't touch them.

Shared Computers

When you are using a shared computer, here are some things to think about:

- Do you know who owns the computer? Do you trust them?

- Do you know who else uses this computer?

- Is the computer set up to record everything you do?

- Is the computer compromised in anyway?

Social Engineering

Most people would call social engineers scam artists. Social engineers set out to trick you into doing something you shouldn't do. They leverage people's desire to be helpful and trusting. They thrive on publicly available information; they use publicly available information to try to convince you that they know you or that they are a friend of yours. This is the main reason why some privacy advocates preach that no one should share anything online. Personally, I believe it is better and more realistic just to stop being so trusting.

People need to realize that someone knowing your sister's name doesn't mean anything. Claiming to know someone or be working on behalf of someone is one of the most common social engineering tricks. Unless that person has personally introduced this stranger, assume they don't really know them.

Even if you have met this person before, that does not mean they are working on anyone's behalf. The only time you can trust that this person is actually working for your boss, for example, is if your boss brings that person to your desk and says something like, "I want you to meet Jane Smith; she is going to be helping me with XYZ, so if she comes to you with something on that, help her out."

Social engineers may call you or send you an e-mail telling some story about how they are in a bind and if you could just do x, y, and z for them, you would be a lifesaver. Those actions typically give them access to some system that they aren't supposed to access. If you are a receptionist, they may visit you in person to gain access to your building. Always validate their stories; don't take anything they say at face value. Be skeptical, think critically, and investigate their claims.

If they claim to be working with or for your boss, call your boss and verify. If they claim to be from the IT helpdesk, call your helpdesk and validate them. If you are a receptionist, follow your guest access policy without exception. No matter what story they tell you, do not take it at face value no matter how hard they tug on your heartstrings. In fact, if they tug at your heartstrings, take it as a red flag that they might be a social engineer trying to trick you. It can also be a red flag if you feel sorry for inconveniencing them. If they come to you with some story that involves them asking for your account password, absolutely refuse, even if you completely validate that everything they are telling you is accurate.

If they are from your company helpdesk or a site administrator, they can reset your password and tell you what they reset it to. If they are not, they have no business knowing your password. If they are from the helpdesk and they really must have access to your account to fix your issue but they can't reset your password, they probably can't fix your problem either. This is an important topic, so I'll be going over it again in the password section.

A Balancing Act

The next topic I need to discuss is the concept that computer security, also known as online security, is a constant balancing act between security/privacy and usability/convenience. One of the core ideas of computer security is that the only computer that is 100 percent secure is powered off, unplugged, and in a vault protected by armed guards. This 100 percent secure computer is also completely useless, and the fact that it is 100 percent secure is pointless. On the other hand, if your focus is on convenience and usability without compromise, then you've automatically eliminated all security. Therefore, to be safe and secure online, you must strike a balance between usability and security while recognizing that it is not possible to ever achieve 100 percent safety or privacy. You must also realize that to be safe and secure online, you'll have to accept some level of inconvenience.

The other aspect of this balancing act has to do with your threat model and the value of what you are protecting. The concept is that if the total value of everything in your house equals $1,000, spending $10,000 on security measures to protect the house does not make any sense. Since the worst case scenario is that you'll lose $1,000, why would you spend $10,000 to protect it? How much you are willing to pay to protect $1,000 is a personal decision. The point here is to think about the value of what you are protecting and how much you are willing to invest in protecting it.

In the online world, for example, if someone hacks your bank account it is going to be much worse than if someone hacks your Netflix account. If someone gains unauthorized access to your Netflix account, there is little they will gain from that and little you will lose. So if you want to tip the scale more towards convenience and worry less about the security of your Netflix account than your bank account, that is perfectly fine. In summary, you can treat all your online accounts with the same security or you can group accounts into security lists and do the balancing differently for each list. It is totally up to you how you decide to do that.

Deleting Files

Did you know that when you delete a file from your computer, it doesn't really go anywhere? First, when you delete something, it goes into the trash or recycle bin on your computer, where you can quickly and easily retrieve whatever you deleted. You can empty the trash, and after that, you can no longer restore files with a few clicks of the mouse. However, whatever you deleted is still not gone. There is readily available software that can undelete whatever you deleted with relative ease. Time for another analogy.

Let's say you manage a large library of books and you have a detailed inventory of every book, including the exact location of the book. For example, your inventory might say that *The Adventures of Tom Sawyer* is on the third floor in the classics section, bookcase ten, shelf five, and slot three on the shelf. Now let's say you receive an e-mail from your boss asking you to purge some of the old books to make room for new books. This e-mail is the same thing as the trashcan on your computer; it merely lists things that need purging.

So you go into your inventory and delete the records for the books that need purging. However, you don't physically remove the books from the shelves, because that's work and you would have to get off your chair and walk around, and that is way too much physical work. Once you receive the new books, you'll remove the old books when you put the new books in their spot. So even though your inventory no longer has any information on several of the books, that doesn't mean the books aren't still there.

Even though you can't find the books using the inventory list, if you are willing to walk around looking for those books, you can still find them. Until, that is, you are forced to remove the old books, either because you need the shelf space for new books or because your boss catches you being lazy and threatens to fire you if you don't remove the old books right away.

This is exactly how the operating system behaves. When a file is put in the trash/recycle bin, it is just tagged for deletion. Once you empty the trashcan, this deletes the inventory record; the file is still on the hard drive until the space it occupies is overwritten by something else.

Undelete programs do a complete inventory of what is on the hard drive and give you a list of things that aren't on the operating system inventory list. You pick what files to undelete, and the software then simply recreates the inventory record.

The security solution to this is a software category called Secure Erase or Crypto Erase. It operates by getting a list of all spots that the inventory says are empty and overwrites those locations with random garbage. This goes back to the previous analogy, for example, a new guy coming in and pulling up a report of empty shelf space, then removing anything that is still in those spots and dusting off all the empty shelf space.

Keep Things Updated

The next concept I'm going to cover is the idea that you should keep everything updated with the latest patches and security updates. The things your employer issues to you from the IT department, if they have one, should take care of it. If they don't, you should take care of it yourself in order to enhance your online safety and security. Your personal electronics are solely your responsibility for keeping up to date.

What does it mean to keep your electronics updated? Well, let me explain. The operating system on your computer, for this audience, is either going to be Microsoft Windows or Apple macOS. All applications that are installed on top of your operating system are called software programs. Both operating systems and applications are written by developers. Since developers are human and all humans make mistakes, all software will have errors and mistakes in it. In the software world, these mistakes are known as bugs. These mistakes often allow malicious applications to do harmful things to your computer. If these mistakes aren't fixed, then a threat actor, like a criminal, can leverage them to take over your computer and do horrible things to it. For more details, see the section on malware.

Once the developer discovers and fixes the mistake, they issue something called a patch or an update. Installing the patch or update fixes the issue on your computer. The best protection against those type of vulnerabilities is to keep your operating system and all your programs updated by installing these patches as soon as they are available. Windows has a feature called Windows Update, which does this automatically for the operating system and its components.

While I am not an Apple Macintosh expert, I believe macOS has the same functionality, just under a different name. This feature, however, does not typically upgrade your operating system between major revisions. For example, I don't know if Windows Update will upgrade Windows 7 to Windows 10, so you may need to do that manually. If you are using an older computer, it is going to be harder to secure it, so, if possible, investing in a new computer has huge security benefits.

This is because after a few years, the developers stop fixing mistakes as they focus on new things. There are a lot of great articles online that show you how to check what operating system you are running and how to check that it is up to date. If you have a Microsoft or Apple store nearby, you may be able to get them to help you.

If you have applications installed, you'll want to make sure those are up to date as well. The good news is that most of the popular and modern software packages have automated update features. That often comes with the requirement that you are using the latest version of their software. Other software may require that you keep abreast of updates from the developer and install them manually. This is obviously more challenging, especially for those without the necessary technical expertise.

The good news is that those without technical expertise are unlikely to be using software without the automated software update. I am a big fan of the subscription model that a lot of the larger software companies are using, compared to paying a single purchase price per version. With a subscription model you know you will always have access to the latest version, and the developer knows they have a steady income stream.

While I have focused on computer software, the same concepts apply to smartphones where the major operating systems are Android and Apple iOS. If you are using a Windows or Blackberry smartphone, you need to research switching to either an iPhone or any of the myriad of Android phones on the market these days. Blackberry and Windows phones are outdated, and keeping them updated and secure is getting harder every day. There are many budget-friendly smartphones available running Android that cost a fraction of the price of the high-end phones. Again, you want to use a relatively new device so that you can get ongoing security updates. As with everything else, research what's best for you.

This idea also applies if you own a tablet, whether it is an Apple iPad or an Android tablet from a company like Samsung, Alcatel, or Lenovo. The good news is that these devices all have an automatic update feature both for apps and for the operating system; just make sure that you allow that auto-update to run frequently. While we often think of smartphones and tablets as something special, in reality they are just small but powerful computers running different operating systems. As I understand it, iOS for iPhone and iPad are similar to macOS, as they are all Apple products, but since I'm not an Apple expert, don't quote me on that.

Then there is this whole field of something called the Internet of Things (IoTs), also called smart devices. These days everything is connected to the internet. For example, your washing machine, your thermostat (e.g., Nest), your doorbell (e.g., Ring), your light bulbs (e.g., Philips Hue), your fridge, and your toaster are connected to the internet these days. I just saw an ad from Pampers about diapers that you can track with your smartphone.

You will know if you have one of those items because you had to configure it to connect to your home network. Anything that connects to your home network and can communicate with the internet is a mini computer that needs to be up to date. If you have an app on your phone to control something in your home, then that item is an IoT. If it can "phone home" to the manufacturer or some service center via the internet, it is an IoT.

Currently in 2019, IoT devices are notoriously bad at security, and their developers aren't diligent about finding and fixing mistakes They seem preoccupied with making the next cool thing. This is naturally a great concern for security professionals. For some of the IoT devices, the worst that can happen is that they become jumping-off points. This means they hide the criminal's tracks and make it look like they are coming from your place. In other cases, there are additional risks.

For example, if a hacker is remotely controlling your toaster, they could override safety protocols and start a fire. If they are controlling your thermostat, they can make it uncomfortable, extremely hot or cold, and spike your utility bill. Right now, the IoT field is very immature and young. As this field develops, hopefully it will get better at security. For now, vigilance, prudence, and attentiveness are in order. If you are not using the "smart" feature of a product, disconnect it from your network. There is not much else you can do at this point in terms of IoT security.

Multiple E-mail Accounts

The concept of maintaining multiple e-mail accounts is, I feel, a bit on the advanced side. Whether that is going to work for you will largely depend on your threat model and how comfortable you are with handling e-mail. If as part of your threat modeling you opted to manage all accounts in the same way and not group things based on their sensitivity, then this may be of limited value to you.

The key is to have separate accounts for each security context. For example, one account that you use exclusively with your most sensitive accounts like banking and other financial institutions. Then another account for your close friends and sites you deem are medium on your sensitivity scale, and one general account that you give out freely to anyone.

Some call this last account their spam account, as they don't care who has this account and it ends up with a ton of spam. The security benefit here is that if one e-mail account is breached, the data loss is contained. An e-mail address is often a crucial part of password recovery functions, so having a well-known e-mail address on sensitive sites can compromise the security level.

For this concept to work, each e-mail address should be distinctly unique so hackers cannot guess your private information. For example, if your spam e-mail account is siggibjarnason@gmail.com, then having your banking e-mail account as siggibjarnason-bank@gmail.com and siggibjarnason-friends@gmail.com as your friends account is not good and jeopardizes your security. Each e-mail address should be totally unique for the best protection. Also, I need to point out that if a site offers the option to use text messages or your phone number for account recovery, always opt for the e-mail option instead. See the authentication section, where I discuss SMS messages and SIM swap fraud to explain this recommendation.

Additionally, I strongly encourage you to utilize the option if your e-mail provider allows you to set up an alias that can only be used as an e-mail address and can't be used to log into your e-mail. The best way to do this is if you can have the account name— the e-mail you sign in with—as an unknown e-mail that no one knows about. Then you can make each of the dedicated e-mail addresses aliases.

I also want to point out that you should include the e-mail account that manages your sensitive e-mails, e.g., financial e-mails, in your sensitive list.

Parts of a URL

Here is something that will come in handy later in the book—the concept of a URL and how to break it down. Let's start by defining what a URL is. The acronym URL stands for Universal Resource Locator. It was designed to help computers find resources on the internet. It's a fancy term for a web address. The resources it is trying to locate can be a variety of things. Some examples of a resource are a web server, a file server, and an e-mail server. It's not important what all of those are; understanding all the different resources available is an advanced topic. The only thing we need to focus on here is the web server resource.

A web server is a computer that serves up your content as you surf the web. Here are a couple of web server URL examples:

https://www.spanishdict.com/conjugate/nadar

https://translate.google.com/#view=home&op=trans late&sl=es&tl=en&text=me%20oyes

These URLs follow specific formatting and are easily interpreted.

- All URLs, regardless of resource type, begin by indicating the resource type.

http:
Web server resource over an insecure connection. HTTP stands for HyperText Transfer Protocol, which is just a method of formatting text with embedded commands for downloading pictures, etc.

https:
This is the same as http, but it uses a secure connection, hence the s at the end.

mailto:
E-mail address.

sftp:
This is a file server and stands for Secure File Transfer Protocol. This is a method of transferring arbitrary files to some computer in the cloud via a secure connection. How this works is an advanced topic outside the scope of this book, as it really has nothing to do with online security. There is also a non-secure version of this (FTP), but this is not recommended.

- The web server resource is followed by two forward slashes (//), then something called a fully qualified domain name or FQDN, followed by another slash (/). Anything following that is a file path on the server or commands to the server. I'll explain this later.

- The e-mail address is the username followed by an @ symbol followed by an FQDN.

Ok, so what is a FDQN? It stands for Fully Qualified Domain Name, or *domain* for short, and it is the address structure for the internet. FQDN structure is a series of components separated by periods. The FQDN structure is read from the end backwards. The FQDN name of translate.google.com is a three-component structure, with .com being at the top of the structure. The top of the structure is called the top-level domain or the TLD. Imagine that: calling the top of the domain the top-level domain. Pretty complex, huh? Back in the early days of the internet, there was a minimal number of TLDs available, and they were supposed to classify the type of organization it belonged to.

.com
Commercial for-profit entities

.edu
Educational institutions

.gov
Governmental institutions

.org
Non-profit organizations

.net
Organization involved in the backbone of the internet

Then, lastly, there's the country-specific TLD if you want to indicate what country you are in instead of the type of organization. I believe the original five TLDs were US-centric, and the country TLD was added as an afterthought when the rest of the world went, "Hey, what about us?" That's just a hypothesis, though.

Today, the number of TLDs is in the hundreds, and the original intentions have lost all meaning.

Anyway, I digress again. The second element in translate.google.com is the organization name—in this case, Google. The third element is a group, department, or product name. In this case, Google Translate is a product offered by Google, which is a commercial entity.

Now, if there are more than three elements to the FDQN, which does happen but not often, just remember to read it from the end backwards. Any additional components are product features or subgroups. For example, account.user.google.com means the account feature of the user product offered by Google, which is a commercial entity.

Now for all the information after the FQDN; that is, product-specific information that is as varied as the grains of sand on a beach. For example:

https://www.spanishdict.com/conjugate/nadar
Establish a secure web server connection to the www product of Spanish Dictionary (abbreviated Spanish Dict.), a commercial organization. Inside that production, go into the conjugation folder and load the conjugation for the Spanish word *nadar*.

https://translate.google.com/#view=home&op= translate&sl=es&tl=en&text=me%20oyes
Establish a secure web connection to the translate product from Google, a commercial organization. Give

```
#view=home&op=translate&sl=es&tl=en&t
```

`ext=me%20oyes` to the product and return the results.

https://www.apple.com.rusky.ru/
Establish a secure web connection to the Russian company (the TLD .ru means Russia) named Rusky, go to the product called com, a feature called apple, and subfeature www. This example will make even more sense after you read the section on scams, cons, and other dangers. Suffice it to say that this has nothing to do with Apple Inc. and is unrelated to the URL https://www.apple.com/

Where Is an E-mail Address Hosted?

Now for a bonus topic that is a bit advanced and that is indirectly related to online security. You can file this under "the more you know." An e-mail hosting company is a type of company that specializes in hosting e-mail accounts and running e-mail servers. The large companies include Gmail, Hotmail/Outlook, and Yahoo. I'm sure you have noticed that only a fraction of e-mails out there contain @gmail.com, @hotmail.com, @outlook.com, or @yahoo.com. Many of them have a company name in the FQDN. So where are those hosted? For example, my e-mail, siggi@infosechelp.net. I'm going to walk you through the steps you can take to find out where any e-mail address is hosted.

Step 1: Go to (https://digwebinterface.com) and enter the FQDN (in my example, infosechelp.net) in the "Hostname" field, select MX for Type, then click the Dig button. If the e-mail address has more than a two-element FQDN, you typically only need the top two.

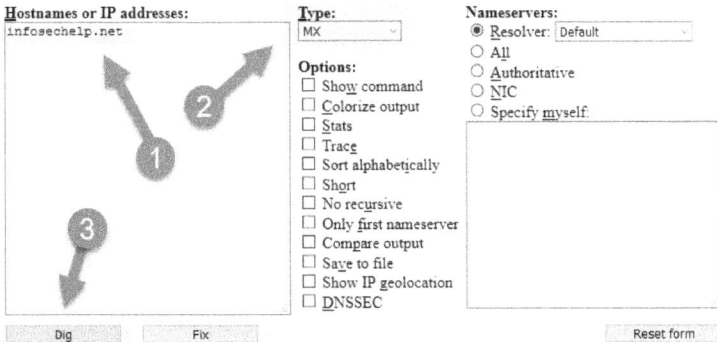

Figure 15: E-mail investigation Step 1

Then, below the Dig button, the results will show:

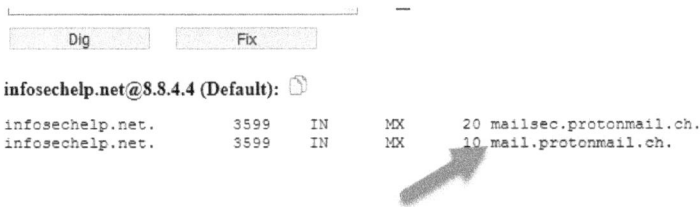

Figure 16: E-mail investigation Step 1 output

In there, you can see that I am hosting my e-mail on a mail server with a company called ProtonMail in Switzerland (TLD .ch). You could Google ProtonMail to find out more, but there is one other step you can take to find out more details. This step is known as a Whois query, and it can tell you what name registered that particular FQDN. Start by going to (https://www.name.com/whois-lookup) and put "protonmail.ch" in the search box.

Figure 17: E-mail investigation Step 2

Name.com is a company that registers domain names in the US, so it's going to try to sell you a domain name registration that is similar to protonmail.ch. Just ignore all of that and scroll down to the Whois lookup for protonmail.ch.

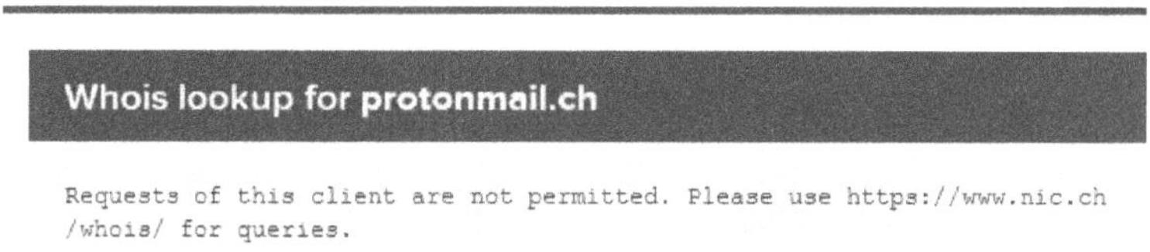

Figure 18: E-mail investigation Step 2 output

Here it says that since this isn't in the US, name.com can't help you, and suggests you try (https://www.nic.ch/whois/), so we'll try that. If a Whois search like this comes up with an unhelpful message, try Googling something like "Whois domain lookup for" and add a space followed by the TLD in question—in this case .ch. When I go to the site that name.com recommended and enter "protonmail" into their search, I get the following information.

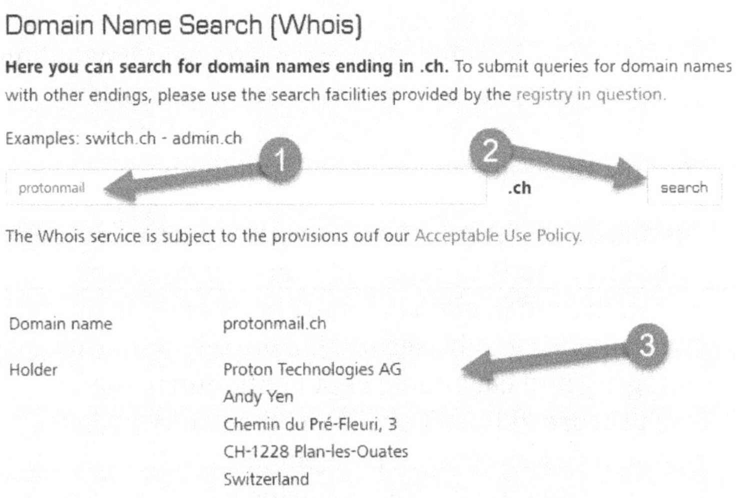

Domain Name Search (Whois)

Here you can search for domain names ending in .ch. To submit queries for domain names with other endings, please use the search facilities provided by the registry in question.

Examples: switch.ch - admin.ch

protonmail   .ch   search

The Whois service is subject to the provisions ouf our Acceptable Use Policy.

Domain name   protonmail.ch

Holder   Proton Technologies AG
                Andy Yen
                Chemin du Pré-Fleuri, 3
                CH-1228 Plan-les-Ouates
                Switzerland

Figure 19: E-mail investigation Step 3

In these results, you can see the officially registered name of the company running ProtonMail as well as the address of the company's headquarters. Amazing what you can find online, isn't it?

CIA and NSA

I am willing to bet that the vast majority of you were intrigued by the terms NSA and CIA in the title of this book and figured that I would dish some conspiracy theory about the US Central Intelligence Agency and the US National Security Agency. Well, those assumptions would be absolutely false but totally expected. I'm not really sorry to crush that expectation.

Regarding NSA, what I was referring to is Network Secure Architecture, which deals with how to connect computers together in a secure manner. The main reason I included the term NSA in the title was to give an example of clickbait, a concept which I will cover in the section on scams. As an everyday online user, you do not need to understand network architecture and how to secure it in order to be safe online; the IT department will handle that.

In this case, CIA refers to the security term *CIA triad*. The CIA triad is the concept that *confidentiality*, *integrity*, and *availability* must be present in order for something to be secure. If a document has no integrity and isn't being kept confidential, then it isn't secure. If it isn't available, the whole point is moot. So a key concept in keeping something secure and private online while ensuring it is also usable means paying attention to all aspects of the CIA triad. Let's investigate these three concepts a little further.

Confidentiality

The Oxford English Dictionary defines *confidentiality* as "The state of keeping or being kept secret or private."

This definition fits very nicely with the way the word is used in computer security. In order to have any privacy and security, you need to be able to keep certain things private and secret. There are many ways to accomplish this.

Sometimes all you need is simply to guard your secrets with access controls – just keep people who don't need to know out of the areas that contain private and secret things. We practice this regularly in the physical world using locks, either on rooms or on containers. Rather than having private stuff lying around on the coffee table in the living room, you put it in a locked drawer in the study, for example. The concept is the same in the computer world; it is just implemented differently.

One method for access control in the computer world is simply to configure the operating system (Microsoft Windows or Apple Mac iOS) with details on who can access what. This is equivalent to your average lock; it keeps most people out, but it can be picked with relative ease. Sometimes you want that extra level of security, so you install a safe inside a locked room. Yes, the safe combination can be cracked, but the difficulty and the time it takes to crack it increases exponentially. So while a skilled thief can pick a door lock in seconds or minutes, it can take hours to crack a high-quality safe, and this requires an entirely different skill level. The computer equivalent of a safe is called "encryption," and I'll explain encryption in more detail later in this book.

Integrity

The Oxford English Dictionary has a few definitions of *integrity*. The first one is about honesty and morals, which doesn't fit our purpose here. The second definition is "The state of being whole and undivided."

This second definition fits our purpose. The dictionary continues with two sub-definitions. The first sub-definition is about structural integrity, while the second sub-definition is "Internal consistency or lack of corruption in electronic data." While both of those sub-definitions portray the correct meaning, it is the second one that is most applicable to our discussion. The corruption referenced in this definition can come from a few different sources.

The storage media can fail, causing the data to become corrupt and unusable. If the data is stored on a magnetic medium, a spurious magnetic field can corrupt the storage medium. Magnetic media are being phased out in the computer world. Today, the only magnetic media that are still in widespread use are traditional hard drives.

However, those are quickly getting phased out too. Those who have been around a computer since the '80s or '90s may remember floppy disks and tape drives, which were magnetic media and which are no longer in use. I am starting to stray into using geeky technical terms which are not important here. The point is that magnetic interference is becoming less of an issue around computers. Magnets and computers used to be a big problem that caused corruption and integrity issues.

Another cause of corruption is intentional user corruption. A disgruntled user has full access to and maliciously changes a document; its integrity has been compromised. If a user who is not supposed to be able to access a document makes an unauthorized change to that document, that document no longer has integrity and should be considered corrupt. This is where confidentiality and integrity come together. If a user who is permitted to read a confidential document but who is not allowed to change it is able to change it, that document now has diminished integrity and confidentiality.

A physical world analogy is when you lock a confidential document in a safe, and when you go to get it later the paper used for the document has degraded. Moisture caused the paper to mold or coffee has been spilled on it, and you can't read the document reliably or at all.

Availability

The final aspect of the CIA triad is *availability*, which is the idea that a confidential document with perfect integrity is not useful or beneficial if you can't access it when you need it. In a physical world scenario, you lock a document in a safe and lock the door to the room with the safe in it. Then you need to access the document and you can't even get to the house which has the room with the safe in it. In this scenario, the document isn't available to you and therefore whether it has integrity doesn't matter. If future availability isn't a consideration—you just want to ensure that the document remains confidential—you should shred the document with a cross-cut shredder, burn the shredded remains, then pulverize the ashes and scatter them over a river. You'll end up with a more secure document that way than by locking it in a safe.

Encryption

Overview

I promised I would explain what encryption is and what it is used for, so I'll do that now. As I mentioned before, encryption is a method for keeping something secret and out of the hands of those who have no business even knowing it exists. The other aspect involves making the secured item available only to those who have a right to have it. The physical world analogy is a safe that someone might install in their house. Encryption is similar to safes, as it comes in various sizes and shapes and with different kinds of locks.

The base concept of encryption involves taking readable text and making it non-readable. The very first known form of encryption is traced back to Julius Caesar, where he used what we now refer to as the Caesar Cipher to secure his correspondence with his army. The basis of this cipher (a cipher is a form of encryption) is to shift each letter by a certain number of positions in the alphabet. To encrypt using the Caesar Cipher using a key of "right 3" you would substitute every A with a D, E with an H, and so on. For example, "RETURN TO ROME" would become "UHWXUA WR URPH." Knowing that that was encrypted using the Caesar Cipher using a key of "right 3" makes reversing the encryption easy.

If you don't know what cipher was used or the key, you will need to do some analysis and try to figure that out. This is referred to as cracking the encryption. People skilled in this area can crack a Caesar Cipher in their head in a matter of minutes; modern computers can crack it in a fraction of second. So obviously we need something stronger and harder to crack.

Modern-day encryption takes the original ciphers and increases the complexity exponentially with the help of advanced mathematics. Current encryption is a complicated mathematical formula that takes human-readable text and renders it unreadable. Then if you know the exact formula used to render the text unreadable and you know the values of the variables used (apologies if anyone is having flashbacks to high school algebra), with those values serving as the encryption password (or the encryption key), you can take that unreadable text and make it readable again.

However, if you don't know the formula or the values (i.e., the key), you may be able to reverse the encryption (i.e., crack it), but it's going to take a while, maybe even a few thousand years. For a physical world analogy, picture having a lock you need to open, but you don't have the key to the lock, you don't know what type of lock it is, and you can't pick the lock. If someone handed you a huge crate full of all sorts of different keys, you might end up finding the right key. If you have to sort through millions of keys, you may be there a while. In the computer security world, trying millions and millions of keys to find the right one is called a brute force attack.

Encryption Types and Categories

Encryptions fall into one of two types: *synchronous* and *asynchronous* encryptions. Each of those can be in one of two categories. Those categories are *encrypting a file* or files (aka a thing) or *encrypting a connection*. Let me dive in and explain further.

Synchronous Encryption

Synchronous encryption is identical to your average physical lock. You have a key to a lock, and you use the same key to lock it and to open it. So if you have the same key or an exact duplication of the key that controls the lock, you can unlock it.

Asynchronous Encryption

The basic concept of asynchronous encryption is a bit more difficult to explain in simple terms as there is no direct equivalent in the physical world, so a certain amount of imagination is going to be required for this. Picture this: someone invented a lock that requires two keys to operate. One key can lock the lock; the other key can only open the lock. The key that locked the lock is not able to unlock it and vice versa. Now let's call the key that locks the safe the *public key* and the key that opens the safe the *private key*. Since the public key is only able to lock the safe, you can hand that key out freely to everyone.

You could even open a network of stores where you can go and pick up a copy of "Joe's Public Key." For this analogy to work for those who are more detail-focused, a little suspension of disbelief is needed. Also imagine, if you will, that this imaginary lock I am talking about is in an unlocked state, and it will accept any public key. Once it is locked with a specific public key, only the corresponding private key will open it. That is in essence how asynchronous (or public/private key) encryption works. Just so you know, private and public keys are the actual technical terms in the world of encryption for asynchronous encryption keys. Asynchronous encryption is kind of like a re-useable inter-office envelope. Once it is sealed, it can only be opened by the recipient; once it has been opened, it can be re-used again, and you can put it in the bin of re-usable secure envelopes for anyone to use.

Encrypting Something

If you are encrypting something, you are locking up and making private something on your computer. This could be an entire drive, a folder on the drive, a document, etc. If you don't know what a drive is, think of it as a storage container on your computer where you store your pictures and documents. You can organize the items on your drive into folders. The analogy here is that the drive is a filing cabinet in your office, and that filing cabinet has hanging folders in it.

You open a drawer in the filing cabinet, pick a folder and either get a piece of paper out or put one in. Whether this drive is built into your computer or a thumb drive is irrelevant. You can also encrypt a USB thumb drive. A USB thumb drive is a little stick you can insert into your computer's USB port and put documents and pictures on it. If you need the contents of that stick to be private and secret, you need to encrypt it, which will turn that stick into a tiny portable document safe. Encrypting something typically uses synchronous encryption; as the user who encrypted the content is typically the user who un-encrypts it, key exchange isn't an issue.

The skillset needed to encrypt documents and other items is beyond the skillset I expect the readers of this book to have, so I'm not going to go any deeper into this aspect of encryption. It is important to be aware of this technology for comprehensive online security awareness. If you have an interest in it or need to use it, you know it exists and can seek training in how to use it.

Encrypted Connections

Before I can explain what an encrypted connection is, I need to explain what a connection is, along with a discussion of what happens when you are using the internet. There is a great free movie on YouTube called "Warriors of the Net" that gives a high-level overview. So if you're up for some extra credit work, go check it out. Here is the direct link (http://www.youtube.com/watch?v=PBWhzz_Gn10). Please note that this was made in the '90s and is fairly dated, with some terminology that's a bit off, but none of that interferes with the explanation of the high-level concepts involved.

So, here are the basic concepts in simple terms. The internet is sometimes called the *world wide web* because in essence every computer is connected together like one big spiderweb. You purchase your internet service from an internet provider such as Comcast, CenturyLink, AT&T, Cox, Wave, etc. They connect your computer to their computers, which in turn are connected to hundreds of other computers and so on. Another way to think of this is that it is similar to the US highway system. All roads are ultimately connected. If you need to drive from your house in Seattle to some house in Atlanta, GA, you need to figure out which roads connect to the roads that will ultimately get you to GA and to that house in Atlanta.

The internet works in a similar fashion; you need to know your originating address and your destination address, then you figure out the best way to get there. Now let's get a bit more abstract and change the metaphor a bit. Let's imagine that instead of wanting to travel to that house in Atlanta, you just want to correspond with them using old-fashioned letters you send through the postal service. You don't care how the letter gets to Atlanta—you just need to get it there.

So you write your letter, address it, give it to the postal worker, and cross your fingers that the letter gets to its destination. Now let's imagine that you are writing a really long letter, but to keep the size of the envelopes small, you only put a couple of pages into each envelope and split the letter into multiple envelopes. To help the recipient put everything together in the right order, you put page numbers on each page.

This is pretty much how the internet works at a very simplified level. If you want to read the news from your favorite news site, you pull up that site in your web browser. What happens in the background is that you are in a way sending that site a short letter asking them to send you a list of today's articles. You will then receive in return a long letter split up among multiple envelopes listing the articles available. You read through that list, pick out an article of interest, and send them another short letter saying, "Please send me article X," back and forth like that.

This back and forth is called a connection. If a postal worker can pick up one of those envelopes, open it up, and read it, that is called an unsecured connection. If you are just reading the news, who cares, right? However, what if you were doing online banking and one of those letters contained all of your checking account transactions? You might not want some random person who works at the post office to read that. This is where a secure or encrypted connection comes into play.

For an encrypted connection, each one of those envelopes is placed into its own super-secure micro safe before it is packaged, addressed, and given to the post office. Now, unless you know how to unlock that safe, you can't see what is in it. So each one of these imaginary envelopes becomes a thing you encrypt. In other words, securing a connection is nothing more than a long string of things that are encrypted in an automated and invisible way.

Now the question becomes: do you use synchronous or asynchronous encryption? Either will technically work. Let's look at the pros and cons of each approach.

Synchronous encryption is fine for a stationary safe example or any case where you can easily and securely exchange the key. If you tried to use synchronous encryption to secure a connection, you would quickly run into the key exchange catch-22 problem. You can't include the key in your box, because what's the point of locking the lock if you leave your key in the lock? Putting the key in a separate unsecure envelope doesn't make sense either, because someone could easily steal the key. So how can you get a key to someone securely without being able to lock it? Therefore, asynchronous encryption is the go-to method for securing a connection. This is because anyone can lock one of those asynchronous locks, needing only your public key, which is freely available. You are the only one who can open it, so no need to exchange keys like in the synchronous case.

You could make synchronous encryption work for a connection between, say, Seattle and Atlanta if you had a secure way to do the key exchange. Let's say the Seattle person and the Atlanta person meet in Dallas and exchange keys in person. Then they go back to their respective locations and now they can securely use synchronous encryption to exchange information long distance, say over the internet. The technical term for this scenario is *pre-shared key scenario*. For most scenarios, the pre-shared key is not practical, which is why asynchronous encryption is more prevalent for encrypted connections.

There are cases where there is a hybrid implementation. In the hybrid scenario, one of the endpoints randomly generates a long, complex, and secure password that they share with the other party over an asynchronously encrypted connection. Then after they have securely exchanged the key, they will establish a new encrypted connection using synchronous encryption, encrypted with the key shared over the asynchronously encrypted connection.

Hashing

There is one other element of encryption to cover— something called a *hash*. I'm in Seattle, WA, as I write this book, so I feel compelled to point out that this type of hash has nothing to do with weed, and you can't smoke this type of hash.

A computer hash is also called one-way encryption; it is a fixed-length string of numbers and letters. A hashing algorithm takes a specific computer file and then generates what's called a hash from that file. There are multiple algorithms out there for hashing, and they all have several similarities.

- It is not possible to reverse the encryption of a hash; therefore it is called one-way encryption.
- For a given algorithm, the output is always the same length. The size or length of the inputted object has no bearing on how long the output is. The algorithm dictates the length of the output. So a hash of a single word is the same length as a hash of 100,000 words.
- For a given algorithm and a specific input file, the output is always the same. For an identical file, I'm guaranteed the same output.
- If a file has extra space in it or has been modified in any way, the output will be drastically different. Older and simpler algorithms have been found to fail in this regard in very rare conditions. The technical term for this is a *hash collision*. If a hash collision is a problem for your personal needs, use a newer collision-free algorithm. I would venture a guess that no one in the core demographic for this book ever intentionally uses a computer hash.

The detail behind each algorithm is beyond the scope of this book. There are two main uses for hashing. First is to validate file integrity. You run a particular algorithm against your file and note the output. Then later, if you want to know if the file has changed, you simply run the same algorithm and compare the results to the results you noted before. If they match, then the file has not changed; otherwise, the file is different. The hash doesn't reveal what was changed, just that a change occurred.

The second use is for properly storing a password so that it is not possible for the site owner to know what your password is. How this works is that when you first provide your password, the site runs that password through a specific algorithm (or recipe), making sure to use salt and pepper and all the proper spices, then they store the results and discard the actual password. When you go to log in, the site uses the same recipe with the exact same spices in the same amounts, and if the results match the saved result, your login is validated; otherwise you are denied access.

Authentication

The first specific topic I'll cover is the concept of *authentication*. This is how you identify who you are online. In the physical world, when you need to identify who you are to another person, you hand that person your government-issued identification card that has your photo, your name, and other pertinent information. The other person verifies the authenticity of the ID and that the picture matches you, reads the relevant information, and then identifies you. In the online world, or just in general, when you are using any sort of machine—like an ATM, for example—it's not that simple. To dig into the concept of machine authentication, I must first explain the concept of authentication factors.

Authentication Factors

Authentication factors are grouped into three categories. In order to have multifactor authentication (MFA), you need to have more than one category involved. Multiple items from the same category is *single-factor authentication*.

The security level is stronger when more factors are involved. This is known as *two-factor authentication* (2FA) if you have two factors involved, or *multifactor authentication* (MFA) if you have more than one factor involved. Often 2FA and MFA are used interchangeably. It is extremely rare to have all three factors involved, so 2FA and MFA are usually the same thing, except in extreme cases.

Unfortunately, today even having two factors is rare. It is crucial for your online safety and security to enable MFA if the site or system supports this. This is one of the best ways to secure your accounts. Some people claim that MFA isn't perfect, so why bother? —to which I respond that nothing is perfect in the world of computer security. Being close to perfect is better than being bad. They are right that enabling MFA doesn't automatically fix all the security issues and make you 100 percent secure. Personally, I'd rather be 90 percent secure than 20 percent secure.

I've never heard any computer security expert proclaim that MFA is perfect. The point of MFA is to enhance your security, not so that you don't have to think about security. Being able to demonstrate that one can bypass MFA controls does not diminish the value of having MFA controls. It gives threat actors one more hurdle, and a difficult one at that, to overcome. As an analogy, adding a second deadbolt to your front door does not make your place immune to break-ins, it just makes it that much harder to break in, at least through your front door.

To be fair, not all MFAs are the same, and it depends on the factor category too.

Authentication Factor Categories

Something You Know
This is something you have memorized or otherwise something you know. This includes usernames, account numbers, personal identification numbers (PINs), passwords, your high school mascot, your first car, your childhood pet, the street you grew up on, and so on.

Most sites rely on a single factor. They may have multistep authentication, but all the items are from the *something you know* category. This is the most insecure category of them all. A threat actor can easily find or guess the answers to the questions. This category is the easiest to implement, the easiest to spoof, and the easiest to replace. If your password becomes compromised, just change it—it's that simple.

Something You Are

This factor deals with the idea that a computer can measure something about you and recognize you. This is also referred to as *biometric authentication*. Some of the things that fall into this category include fingerprints, retina scans, iris scanners, palm scanners, and facial recognition. There have even been attempts to use the way you walk and the way you type as biometric factors, with limited success. Again, you get the idea.

The *something you are* category is very secure when implemented correctly but is frequently implemented incorrectly in a way that is easy to spoof, for example, when someone fools a facial recognition system with a photo. Even when implemented correctly, a criminal with the right skills, motivation, and resources can beat biometric authentication. Spoofing this category requires significant time and resources, so only the most sophisticated and dedicated criminals will even attempt it.

The bad part is that it is hard to replace anything in this category. For example, how exactly do I reset my fingerprints? What about changing my iris or retina? That sounds like it would require changing my eyeballs, and that does not sound like fun. Not to mention undergoing plastic surgery so that your face looks different. In short, this category is hard to implement, impossible to replace, and difficult to spoof or bypass.

Something You Have

These are physical objects you have on you, and you can prove possession of them. For example, this could be the card you insert into the ATM. If you work for the US government or are a member of the US military, then you will have a Common Access Card (CAC) to use on their computers. CACs are also called smart cards. A smart card is something that you insert into a computer that the computer can read. There are apps for your smartphone, called authenticators, that display a number for you to type in to prove that you physically have your phone. I'm sure you get the idea.

This last category, *something you have*, I would argue is the most common MFA factor in use today. While it requires more effort to implement than the *something you know* category, it is easily understood and not that hard to deploy. Either it works or it doesn't. Unlike biometrics, implementing this incorrectly is rare. If you lose it or it becomes compromised in some way, you can either reset it or get a new one. A bit of a pain but not bad; you might be out 50 dollars, but no surgery necessary.

Depending on the exact thing you have, the difficulty of bypassing it will vary. Typically, to compromise one of these factors, you must phish or social engineer the holder or you must steal it. So it's doable with minimal resources and a fair amount of effort. In short, medium-difficult to deploy, medium-easy to replace, and hard to spoof. There are four subcategories. In order of least secure to most secure, here they are:

1. **SMS/text message MFA.** If your phone number becomes compromised, so are all sites that utilize SMS for the second factor.

2. **Smartphone application authenticators.** These can be compromised via phishing and other social engineering. This can work over the phone, when a scam artist calls you up and convinces you to read the number to them and they can use it. Theoretically, it might be possible to compromise the smartphone in order to compromise the authenticator, although I have not heard of this happening.

3. **Hardware random number tokens.** These operate in the same manner as smartphone authenticator applications except that they are dedicated separate pieces of hardware with only one function—to show the number. I am classifying these as more secure, as they don't have any attack vectors other than phishing or social engineering. They have no user interface and no way to connect them to anything. They have all of the same social engineering weaknesses. While they don't have any attack vectors, the likelihood of losing these is higher than that of losing your smartphone. Also, you cannot secure these in the event of loss unless you can remotely disable them.

4. **CAC, smart cards, and FIDO U2F-/FIDO2-certified USB keys.** These are physical things

you must insert into the computer you use in order to authenticate. Unless you have the registered card on you, there is nothing you can do to authenticate through it. Therefore, these are immune to social engineering attacks. Even if you wanted to help someone remotely log into an account that is protected by one of these, you can't. So unless you steal the registered card or key, you are out of luck. I am not aware of any cases where an account protected by one of these has been compromised, and they are known to be very secure and hard to intercept or bypass. I am guessing that that is why all US Department of Defense accounts use common access card (CAC) protection, which is a combination of a smart card and an ID badge. The biggest threat to these is the user losing them, in which case they could fall into the wrong hands. FIDO-type USB keys are very similar in nature to CAC and smart cards. Smart cards are in credit card or ID badge form. FIDO-type USB keys are, as the name implies, in the same form as USB thumb drives.

SMS MFA

Some sites will offer you two-factor authentication (2FA) by sending you a text message with a number, and that number has a short expiration time (when implemented correctly). This falls into the *something you have* category, so it is a true 2FA, but it is the least secure 2FA option because voice calls and text messages can be intercepted, copied, and redirected. The easiest way to accomplish this is the method known as a SIM swap scam. A SIM is a little card that the cell phone carrier puts into your phone to register it with the company's network.

The great thing about the SIM card is that when you buy a new phone, you don't have to contact your carrier; you just take the SIM out of the old phone and put it into a new one. The bad thing about this is that it creates new vulnerabilities. The SIM swap scam utilizes social engineering and involves convincing your cell phone company that you have lost your phone and asking them to replace your existing SIM with a new SIM. If they are successful, they now control your phone number, and any text messages you receive now go to the criminal who stole your phone number. To make matters worse, your phone no longer works. So this compromises all site logins that use text messages as a 2FA.

FIDO U2F USB Keys

The best option is to use a FIDO Universal 2-Factor (U2F)-certified USB key. This is like a smart card but utilizes the USB form for ease. The Yubico website defines U2F as an open authentication standard that enables internet users to securely access any number of online services with one single security key instantly and with no drivers or client software needed.

The website also states that Google and Yubico created U2F with support from NXP and the vision to bring strong public-key cryptography to the mass market. Today, the FIDO Alliance, an open-authentication industry consortium, hosts the technical specifications. I know there are some technical terms in those quotes, but hopefully you'll understand them better after completing this book.

This type of USB key is the most secure option as long as you don't lose the key. YubiKey 5 NFC offers the most complete feature list but is also the most expensive (around $45 each in February 2019). Other options are available that have a subset of the same features and they are less expensive. Whether this is easier or harder to set up than authentication apps I think is debatable and depends on the user and their situation. The possibility of the user losing this or not having it readily available seems higher than with authentication apps, but there is no debating how secure it is. Unfortunately, very few sites support it today.

Authentication Apps

Another great option, which is popular and easy to use, is an authentication app on your phone. An authentication app is an app that is synced to a particular site and that displays a rotating number every 30–60 seconds. When you sync the app to a specific site, there is a secret variable exchanged, which is unique to each user. When you factor this secret into a time-based formula, you have a number-generation system that is unpredictable to everyone except the site in question.

So if you can provide the correct number at the correct time compared to what the site is expecting, you have proven that you have the right authentication app. There are many authentication apps out there. Here are some examples:

- Google Authenticator

- Microsoft Authenticator

- LastPass Authenticator

- Entrust ST

- Symantec VIP

- RSA SecureID

- Authy

- Duo Security

Unfortunately, it's up to the site owner what form of authentication factors they support; typically, users can't influence the site owners.

The three apps with "authenticator" in their name plus Authy all support the same protocol, so if a site supports one of them, it is highly likely that any one of them will work. For example, I use Authy on all the websites that support Google Authenticator. As far as Entrust, Symantec, RSA, and Duo are concerned, they all have a proprietary approach and are not compatible with each other.

How an authentication app works is that you install the app on your smartphone and then you register it with a site that supports that app. How the registration for an authentication app works will vary depending on the protocol. For the authenticator protocol used by Google, Microsoft, Authy, and LastPass, the site will show you a QR barcode that you scan with your smartphone. So, in a way, you are registering the site with the app.

The information in the QR code allows the app to synchronize with the site and exchange that secret I mentioned before, which is embedded in the QR code. For the other protocols, the app will show you information that you enter into the website's 2FA registration screen. I think Entrust is the only one that does both. You start by entering information from the app; then the site gives you a number to enter into the app. For the final step in the registration, you will have to provide the number currently displayed on the screen so that it can verify that things are in sync.

Once you have synchronized the app and the site, in order to log in you provide the username and password as usual, then you are asked for the number in your authentication app. If the number you type in matches what the site was expecting, it logs you in. Otherwise, it boots you out. What makes this more secure than SMS (text message) 2FA is that you must gain access to the account before you can take over the 2FA. If someone can accomplish that, they've only compromised that one account.

General Authentication Factor Overview

Now, as I covered earlier, security comes at the price of convenience, and this is no exception. If all you need is what is in your brain, logging into your accounts is easy and convenient. Then again, not having to log in is more convenient. Having to use an authenticator app on your phone is a bit of pain, but you always have your phone with you, so it's not a big deal. Having to get your wallet or your key chain when you need to log into something is more of a pain. This also doesn't speak of the inconvenience involved in setting one of those up, which is relatively minor.

Some organizations misunderstand the concept of MFA. If you are asked for your username, password, your mother's maiden name, and the name of your best friend in 11th grade, that is just inconvenient single-factor authentication, as those are all things you know. Having multiple things from one category isn't multifactor authentication. If an organization only utilizes the *something you know* factor, having more questions to answer is better than nothing, but not much. It will only deter the laziest criminals. Later in this book, I'll go into detail about what you can do to make this more secure (spoiler: lie your ass off).

The most common authentication method is to use a username and password. If you can add to that method by using a smart card, for example, then you have now exponentially improved the security of your system. Now it is not enough to guess the right answer to some questions in order to compromise the system. The hacker also needs to steal the smart card. This is possible if the criminal is dedicated, so this is not perfect, but close to perfect and so much better than just using username and password authentication. Most criminals—and most threat models—aren't willing to go any further than trying to obtain your username, password, and the answers to the security questions.

If you add a fingerprint reader as well, you engage all three factors. Now a criminal must know (or guess) your username and password, steal your smart card, and have your fingerprint (or have the technology to fake your fingerprint). The criminal would have to be super motivated to go to all that effort.

Furthermore, if a criminal does steal your finger, you'll notice that and might notify someone, plus it tends to be a bit messy. Once you know that someone is trying to compromise your account, you can inform the administrator, at which point they'll disable your account, making all the efforts of the criminal useless. If your account is disabled and you cannot log in, neither can the criminal.

Therefore, multifactor authentication exponentially increases your security, and each additional factor is another exponential increase. When a threat actor only needs to have your username and password and know where you went to high school, that is possible for most criminals. Yes, having to find out what high school you went to may be annoying to them, but it will only slow them down slightly, and only the laziest criminals are deterred.

All they need to do is look you up on Facebook and they'll have their answer. Very few criminals can manufacture fingerprints or are willing to go to the effort of stealing your smart card. Additionally, cutting off fingers is crossing the line for many criminals.

If you're on a site you want to secure but all it offers are security questions, then the best advice I can give you is to treat the security questions as extra passwords. The last thing you want to do is to give the real name of your friend when the security question asks for the name of your best friend in grade school. You want to give a fake answer like "walking tick red." More on this idea in the section on passwords. Also, check out the section on password managers to learn how to track your fake security answers.

I strongly advise that on any sites you classify as needing high security, you look at and enable any 2FAs or MFAs that the website offers. If a site only offers single-factor authentication, see if you can pressure them into providing a multifactor option; however, in most cases this will not be successful. If that fails, re-evaluate your use and classification of that site. For the record, I have enabled this on all sites I use that support it, regardless of my classification of the website.

Password Selection and Handling

Now that I've covered what authentication factors are and the benefits of having additional factors, let's discuss what makes a good password and proper password handling. The term *password* is not accurate; it should be passphrase, because using just one word is incredibly insecure. Unfortunately, we are stuck with the term password. If you were to use a simple English dictionary word as your password, then someone could compromise that account in a fraction of a second. When you string together a phrase of multiple unpredictable words, it can take hundreds or thousands of years to compromise that password, which is more time than most hackers are willing to invest.

Plus, you might change the password during that time. The key here, though, is the unpredictable part.

If your password is "SeattleSeahawksAreTheBest" and you are well known for being a huge Seattle Seahawks fan, it won't take long at all to guess your password; in fact, it will probably be guessed within one or two tries. Now, if you are a Dallas Cowboys fan and known for your hatred of the Seattle Seahawks, then that phrase is more unpredictable and more secure. The fact that it is about football still makes it somewhat predictable. The best thing to use is a nonsensical phrase—something like "thecowjumpmoonplayingpiano." That is the most nonsensical phrase I can think of at the moment, but the point is to string together some words that you would never see together in a typical sentence. Or at least make the sentence something you are unlikely to use. For example, make a phrase about something you never talk about, so even those who know you well would never guess it. We all have a lot to draw from there. Also, the longer the better.

When I talk about cracking or compromising a password, I'm not talking about the criminal using the login screen for the site to guess your password. That method is too slow and generates too much noise to be a practical approach for a criminal. Typically, a threat actor will compromise the entire site and steal their complete user database. Then they will have the user database on their own computer and will try to guess everyone's passwords as fast as their computer will allow without anyone knowing. Therefore, changing your passwords periodically is a good thing.

Early on, I covered the concept of hashing and how a well-written site will use hashing with some salt to properly store users' passwords. While a hash is not reversible, you can play a guessing game to figure out what the password is. As a kid, you may have played this game with your parents or siblings. There was something you wanted to know that they wouldn't tell you, so you kept making random guesses and watched their reactions to see if you guessed correctly. This is precisely how offline password cracking, or hash cracking, works. It's called offline hash cracking because the threat actor has all the password hashes and tries to guess them without even being on the internet, or online.

A threat actor has a program that guesses a password and uses the hash formula and the salt specified to see if the hash they generated matches any of the hashes they just stole. Of course, what formula to use and what salt to specify is a guessing game too. Remember, when you run the same value through the same hashing calculation you are guaranteed to end up with the same output. The hash-cracking software can make hundreds of millions of guesses per second, which is why it can crack a predicable password in no time at all.

Once the threat actor has guessed the correct password, they can take over your account without you even knowing—unless, of course, you have MFA enabled. Since cracking your password is really just a guessing game, the trick is to make sure no one can guess your password, even if they have hundreds of billions of guesses. Or as the kids say, "You'll never guess it in a billion years". In a billion years, hopefully, you'll have changed your password anyway.

One of the many great federal government agencies here in the US, is called the National Institute of Standards and Technology, or NIST. This institute is charted with setting and publishing standards and recommendations in the broad field of Technology. Their website says their vision is to "be the world's leader in creating critical measurement solutions and promoting equitable standards. Our efforts stimulate innovation, foster industrial competitiveness, and improve the quality of life."

NIST publishes a lot of standards relating to computers as part of the technology field. One of these standards is called Special Publication 800-63, or SP800-63 for short. That is such a clever and memorable name, right? Those government types can be so creative. Anyway, SP800-63 is a very technical document filled with various technical recommendations related to computer security. One of the recommendations provides guidance on passwords and password rules. NIST used to say, that the most important aspect of a password was its complexity. Did it have uppercase and lowercase letters, did it have special symbols, and did it have numbers?

According to this advice, a password of P@ssw0rd was supposed to be a cryptic and secure password, or at least that is how some people interpreted it. This turned out to be horrible advice that ended up being completely reversed. In May of 2016, NIST released a draft update to SP800-63 for public comments. In June of 2017, version three of SP800-63 was officially published. In the third revision,

NIST completely changed their stance on their password guidance.

A respected cybersecurity blog named Naked Security, by a computer security product company named Sophos, published an article that does a good job of summarizing the changes. The main thing that is applicable here, is that they are now saying length is king when it comes to good passwords and no more rules about complexity. Links to articles for further reading are in the reference section in the appendix section at the end of the book.

With that history and commentary out of the way, let's get practical. The first thing to think about is, that you want to have a separate password for every site. I like to compare passwords to underwear, it is never acceptable to share them, and changing them from time to time isn't a bad idea either. There are two absolutes regarding passwords that you should never deviate from if you want to maintain good online security, and they both involve the word *share*.

The first rule is to never share passwords between sites. Your Facebook password should be completely different from your Twitter password, and neither should have any resemblance to your Gmail password. In other words, each site you log into should have an entirely unique password.

The other concept is to avoid sharing your passwords with anyone. Under no circumstances should you tell your passwords to anyone, ever—no exception. Just don't do it, like, at all. Absolutely just no, like so totally like nope, no way. Any "But what if

...?" or "What about ...?" questions relating to sharing a password should all be answered with an absolute and unconditional hard no, and don't do it. Any questions? Good—moving on.

(Sorry about the valley girl impression. Trying to keep things light.)

If you decide to make exceptions to either of these absolutes, then just make sure that you are following your threat model and your privacy stance and that it supports your approach to balancing things. Also, make sure you've thought through your risk and reward balance and that you're clear on your reasons for breaking this unbreakable rule. Breaking either of those absolutes about password sharing can have a severe risk of jeopardizing your online security and privacy, so please avoid it at all costs.

Why is sharing a password always such a hard no? That is very easy to answer. Sharing a password with another person will allow them to operate online as if they were you. This could have a lot of unforeseen consequences. You are giving them permission to impersonate you. Like teaching someone to forge your signature and giving them permission to do so. What could possibly go wrong with that? Everyone should have their own login and operate under their own identity.

If your Facebook and Yahoo password is the same password as your bank and many other sites and your Facebook or Yahoo account gets compromised, the criminal has access to all the sites that use that password. If each site has its own password, if one site is compromised, no other site is impacted.

I'll go into more details in the section on scams, but I thought it was important to touch on it here as another reason for never sharing your password with anyone. One of the popular scams is when you get a phone call or e-mail claiming to be from tech support or your employer's IT department telling you that in order to fix something, they need your password. Never under any circumstances should you give your password to anyone like that. The proper response to a request like that is, "Please reset my password and let me know what you've changed it to." If they are really from tech support or IT, they should have no problem doing this. If they give you pushback on this, they are either so utterly clueless that they can't fix your problem, or they are a criminal trying to take over your account.

So you lose nothing by refusing, and you gain everything by maintaining the security of your account. Even if you call tech support for some problem you are having, never give them your password. If they insist, either live with the problem or delete your account. Being on a site with that bad a security practice means that they are probably already compromised by a threat actor. For the record, I can't think of any case where tech support would have a legitimate need for your password, and I've been in IT for over 30 years. In the rare case that they can actually justify it, make them reset it.

Now, if you are worrying about how to keep track of all those unique passwords for dozens or hundreds of sites, no worries; I've got your back. An upcoming chapter on password managers will tackle that problem and help you manage your passwords.

As I said before, a longer password is better; even NIST has reversed its advice on complexity and is going strictly with length. Many sites are still stuck on the old advice, so you may need to adapt. If the site will allow it, selecting a password that is longer than 20 characters is advisable. If 20 characters is too long, try to make it longer than 14 characters.

The reason why you want your password to be longer than 14 characters is something called the LANMAN hash. When Microsoft first introduced authentication into Windows back in the late 1980s and early 1990s, they introduced this thing called LANMAN that allowed Microsoft computers to interconnect and authenticate each other. The LANMAN hash was limited to 14 characters and could be cracked by your average desktop in a matter of minutes, regardless of how complex you made it.

When Microsoft first started securing computers, cybersecurity wasn't really important yet. There was not a lot of information about how to secure computers properly, so this authentication scheme turned out to be incredibly insecure. In order not to interfere with the older products, Microsoft kept this authentication scheme in Windows products. So by using a password that is longer than 14 characters, you are ensuring that the site isn't using this old, outdated authentication scheme. If a site limits you to 14 characters, be afraid, be very afraid.

For me, instead of being satisfied with 15 characters, I shoot for a random length somewhere in the 20s or 30s or even longer. It is worth noting that I've come across several sites that limit you to 20-character passwords. For those sites, I choose something that is 15–20 characters long. Using a genuinely random 25-character string is better than using a phrase that is 25 characters long. The difference is that a 25-character phrase might be compromised in anywhere between days and hundreds of years, depending on how predictable it is, and a truly random string with special characters and numbers might take tens of thousands of years. A good password manager application will have a random password generator.

Either way, I'm not worried if I'm using a truly unpredictable phrase. Doesn't matter how long or complicated your password is, if someone who knows a few things about you can just guess it correctly in a couple of tries, it is not secure. As I discussed before, for example, if you are huge Seahawks fan and everyone knows that you never miss a game, then a passphrase involving Seahawks and football is probably ill-advised. Also, you may want to stay away from using Seattle or well-known Seattle landmarks in the password if you live in that area. Same goes for landmark names of areas you are well known for visiting. Using the name of the site in the password is a terrible idea as well. Again, those are very predictable things.

Here is a good comic from the famous xkcd website that summarizes this idea.

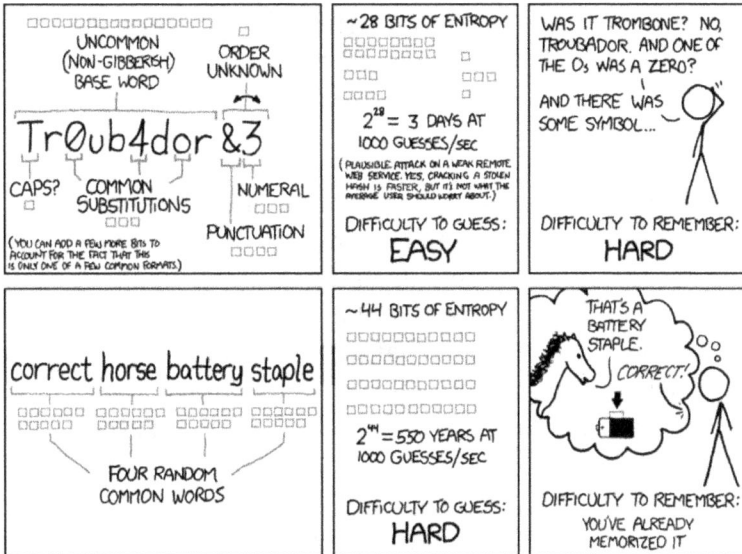

Figure 20: xkcd comic on passwords

You can find this comic at (https://xkcd.com/936/). If you don't know, entropy is basically a measure of randomness.

Previously, I talked about those dreaded questionnaires that sites think are security questions and which they mistakenly believe provide 2FA. I just want to reiterate that giving truthful answers to those questions weakens your security instead of enhancing it as the site creators mistakenly believe. The way to work around that is to make the answer as absurd and far from the truth as possible. If you are known for disliking Star Trek, you could say that Captain Picard, the captain of the *Starship Enterprise*, was your best friend, or something like that. Better yet, just fill those answers with a random string of characters, then store the answer in your password manager.

Managing Passwords

Earlier, I alluded to the problem of managing dozens or hundreds of unique passwords, and that is absolutely a massive problem with maintaining a secure online presence. The solution to this problem is something called a password manager. A password manager will help you manage your passwords. How's that for a 100 percent correct but pretty useless definition? A password manager comes in many forms, and I'll cover many of them here shortly. A password manager, generally speaking, is just a tool that helps you track all your passwords. It's anything from a physical notebook to a fancy application. In essence, a password manager is something where you store your usernames, passwords, and answers to security questions for all your sites, enabling you to have unique passwords and security answers for every website.

Different forms have different pros and cons. There are three critical features needed from all password managers, and it involves the CIA triad I discussed earlier. Whatever password manager you choose, it needs to be available to you whenever you are logging into sites and applications, and it needs to ensure that only authorized people can access it while ensuring data integrity. Additionally, think about the balancing act while reading the comparison. Remember there is no such thing as perfect security; it's all a matter of how you balance things.

Lately, there have been articles online talking about how password managers aren't perfect and how under the right circumstances they can be compromised. My response to those articles is the same as to the naysayers on MFAs—that nothing in cybersecurity is perfect. It's good that researchers are finding these problems, as this allows the vendors to fix them. All the issues I've seen lately are such outliers that if you find yourself in a scenario where one of those flaws can be exposed and leveraged, you've got bigger problems to worry about.

For example, I was just reading an article about how a threat actor can get your password by installing malware on your computer that can read the memory of the computer and send the info back to the criminal. If you've got malware like that on your computer, it doesn't matter what precautions you've taken, the criminal will have all your account information whether or not you use a password manager. A type of malware called keyloggers or spyware, which I'll cover later, is a lot easier to pull off than decoding memory locations. In short, what they do is record all your keystrokes, clipboard, etc.

Some say to stay away from tools that have been breached. I disagree. Experiencing a breach can be good or bad depending on the details of the breach, and how they responded to the breach says a lot about the company and the security of the product. For example, if a company was breached but no data was lost, that speaks positively about the security of the product. It says that just because a criminal can breach the outer perimeter, they won't have free rein of their systems, which happens frequently. If they respond quickly and fix the hole the criminal was able to breach, it means that they take security seriously. I would rather do business with a company that suffered a breach, didn't lose any data, and fixed the issue right away than with a company that has never had a breach.

Then there are random people out there claiming to be experts and saying that password managers are useless because they aren't perfect. They talk about how you shouldn't put all your eggs in one basket, and instead just have one really good password and use it everywhere. Those people clearly don't understand cybersecurity. The amount of bad advice out there that is phrased to sound correct is staggering. Let's discuss this bad advice and analyze its pieces. So instead of trusting a single well-vetted resource or company with all your various account information, you share all of your account information with hundreds of totally unvetted companies.

That makes no sense at all. I'll refer you back to the rule about sharing passwords for more details on why this is incredibly bad advice as well as my earlier commentary about MFA and people who don't seem to understand cybersecurity. If the basket is built well with proper protection, then putting all your eggs in that basket isn't a bad thing. Especially if it is specifically designed to protect eggs. It's better to have all your eggs in one basket than to have them lying on the floor where someone can easily step on them.

I imagine that those that are criticizing password managers, MFAs, and others are the same people who tell others:

- Not to get a fire extinguisher because they might use it wrongly. Plus, once your house is fully engulfed, a fire extinguisher isn't going to do you any good.

- Not to install a smoke detector because if you forget to replace the battery, it's not going to do you any good.

- To drive without a seatbelt because you might need to get out of the car in under five seconds and the seatbelt will just slow you down. You might even get tangled in the seatbelt trying to escape.

- Why even bother wearing a helmet? It can't guarantee that you won't get killed.

I'm sure each of you knows a few more examples of bad advice from your circle of friends.

With all that out of the way, let's talk about various types of password manager. Again, remember that there is no such thing as one size fits all. None of these options are always right or always wrong; it always depends.

Physical Password Managers

Some might call this the old-school solution, and for many, it is the simplest and easiest solution. It is simply a physical paper notebook where you write down the details of each site and the login information. My parents call this their bible, as it contains all the information that is critical to them, including people's names, addresses, and phone numbers. Whether this is the right solution for you depends on several factors, including your threat model. Here are some things to consider

- Confidentiality: Can you ensure that no unauthorized people can get their hands on your notebook? The answer to this is highly dependent on your threat model and your lifestyle.

- Integrity: Can you safeguard the notebook from damage? Damage from water, fire, and also misplacing the notebook tend to be the greatest threat to a physical notebook.

- Availability: Is this notebook going to be handy and convenient when you need to log into a site? If you only own one computer and that is the only place you ever log into anything, having a notebook next to it isn't going to be an issue. If you have a laptop that you move around and travel with, you need to make sure the notebook goes wherever the laptop goes and that you keep it secure.

The biggest threat to this type of password manager is losing it, having it stolen, or misplacing it. If you don't think this will be a problem and you are happy with the availability and integrity problem outlined above, then you can use this method. There will be people who criticize this method; don't let them deter you.

Sticky Notes

Using sticky notes is probably the worst way to manage your passwords. This involves writing them down on sticky notes and sticking them to your monitor. This is equivalent to putting up a key rack on the outside of your house. With this method, you are eliminating all balance, just going solely with convenience, and abandoning all security. If this is you, please get a notebook, put your sticky notes in them, and secure the notebook.

The Notepad

This comes close to the sticky notes method, and you should avoid it as well. It is a slight improvement, though, as now you've relocated the key rack from outside your house to right inside a door that may or may not be locked. The notepad method doesn't necessarily mean using the notepad application, but generally that is what happens. The user uses their favorite application for note-taking or text-editing and they simply type all their account information into it. Now if anyone gets their hands on your computer, or even just the files from the computer, they'll have access to all your accounts. If this is you, consider upgrading to a password manager application.

Password Manager Applications

With this method, you are using an application that is specifically designed to help you manage your passwords. This type of application is designed to store your passwords and all the associated information in a highly secure manner using strong encryption. The best ones use the strongest encryption possible, and in some cases, multiple layers of encryption, where you encrypt the encrypted message. This is like putting something into a locked box, then you put that locked box inside a portable safe, which you put into a floor safe that is inside of a bank vault. Just like a Russian doll, you break through one layer only to be rewarded by another layer of encryption. Or in a physical example, you pick one lock only to find another lock to pick.

You need to be careful when selecting a password manager application. Just like any other application, make sure you are using a product from a reputable company. Just like fake malware and virus scanners are actually just viruses or malware, there are applications out there posing as password managers attempting to collect your account information. In addition to researching the company, do some research to make sure they've taken security seriously and that you can trust them with your account information.

Password managers are local only, or online hybrids. Online password managers tend to offer local caching to help with the availability issue when you are offline. For all password managers, you need to specify a secure password to encrypt the storage file. The security of the application depends on how secure your password is. With a password manager, the only password you actually have to know is the application password. All other passwords you store in the application and you don't have to worry about them. Also, some password managers are more properly described as secret managers, as they allow you to store secure notes, addresses, and credit card information.

Here are more details:

Local Password Managers

A local password manager, as the name implies, is installed locally on a specific computer. Passwords are stored in a heavily encrypted file on that computer. This means that you must be on that specific computer to have access to your account info. This is very similar to using a physical notebook. If you only access the internet from one computer and you can secure that computer in a way that meets the needs of your threat model, then this might be a good solution for you. There is still the issue of ensuring the integrity of the data file. If that file becomes corrupt or is accidentally deleted, then you've just lost your entire password book.

You can back up the data file, but then you must safeguard that data somehow. Putting it on a thumb drive that you store in a safe might be a good option if you can make sure you keep it up to date. If you put a copy of the data file on a thumb drive and it gets into the hands of a criminal, now that criminal has all your account information, assuming they can crack your password. This is like losing a copy of all your keys in public and a criminal picking them up. Not a good situation.

While the data file is encrypted, if a threat actor gets hold of it, they can work on brute-forcing the password. If you recall, brute-forcing a password is a guessing game. Threat actors have software that can guess the password a hundred million times per second, and it's only a matter of time until they guess the right password. If the password is more difficult, like 30 random letters, it may take a few hundred years, but eventually they will guess it. If it is easy to guess, it will take a shorter time. The bad thing is that you can't change the password after you've lost the file.

One of the significant shortcomings of a local password manager is that they typically do not offer any sort of an MFA option, as these all require online access. Also, they don't provide any kind of defense or notification for bad passwords or login attempts, because if a threat actor has your file and is trying to crack it, then you have no way of knowing. Additionally, I find local password managers to be more complicated than online ones as they require more configuration. For an installed application, you must typically specify all sorts of configuration items, including where to store the database, what to call it, what level of encryption to use, and whether you want compression or not. For an inexperienced user, these are confusing questions that tend to get answered with a *whatever, just do the thing* attitude. This can lead to a less than secure database. Also, you are completely in charge of securing your data file, and you have no one to rely on to help you with that. This is a big obstacle for some users.

On the plus side, all that configuration allows you more flexibility; advanced users may appreciate being able to configure things just the way they like.

Also, you are completely in charge of securing your data file, and you don't have to trust anyone else. This is a big plus for some users.

If you access the internet from more than one device, like your laptop, phone, or desktop, then you must figure out how to keep your password vault available. You need to decide where to install the application and how to have access to it when it is needed. You could install the application on all the different devices and figure out how to sync the data between them, but this could introduce security issues. You could find an application that allows for installation on a thumb drive; those applications are called portable applications. As long as all the devices you use have thumb drive access, this should work for you. The significant threats with having the data on a thumb drive include losing the drive or drive corruption. By the way, just because an application is marketed and bears all the hallmarks of a locally installed application does not mean that it doesn't have an online component. I'll go into the details of various malware later. One type of malware is called Trojan, a reference to the Trojan horse in Greek mythology. Trojan malware pretends to be one thing and does something completely different. For example, a Trojan might look and function like a locally installed password manager and then secretly send all of your info to the criminal author. I know I alluded to this before, but it bears repeating.

As I mentioned before, make sure the password manager author is reputable and that the application has been designed to secure your data effectively. Just because the author claims it is secure doesn't mean it is secure. With this, as in many cases before, research and critical thinking is your best course of action.

A popular application in this category is called KeePass. It is a free, open source OSI Certified application that security personnel use and recommend. This is one of the rare exceptions where something that's free is not questionable. KeePass is donation based and created solely to help others to be more secure. If you want a local password manager and don't have the time or energy for a lot of research, I recommend you go with KeePass. You can find KeePass here (https://keepass.info/).

Online Password Managers

Online password managers operate under a model that in the computer world is known as Software as a Service (SaaS). What that means is that the software is running in the cloud instead of locally on your computer. In case you are wondering what the cloud is, we're not referring to those white puffy things in the sky. It is simply the internet. Someone thought it would be clever to rebrand the internet as the cloud. So with an online cloud- or internet-based password manager, you access, change, and add entries through a website.

This means a few different things.

- There is nothing you must install in order to use and access your data.

- Typically, there is nothing to create or configure.

- Your data is accessible anywhere you have internet connectivity.

- Unless this online password manager has an offline feature where the information is cached locally, if you don't have internet access, you can't access your information.

- You are trusting a third party to ensure the confidentiality, integrity, and availability of your password database (your notebook, if you will).

- Someone else is ensuring the safety of your password database, and as long as you trust them, you don't have to worry about it.

The last few points need additional discussion. To begin with, password managers with an online component require the highest level of trust, and thus it is critical to ensure the developers of that tool are trustworthy and reputable.

As I mentioned in the local password manager section, trust is paramount when it comes to password managers of any sort. When using an online password manager, you are outsourcing to a third party the task of making sure that only those you authorize have access to it. Additionally, you are trusting that they will keep it free from corruption and other integrity issues as well as ensuring that it is always available to you when you need it. It is very important to research thoroughly when you are choosing your password manager.

To help with the availability component, you should expect there to be an installed application that keeps a local copy and keeps it synchronized with the online version. This process is called caching. This means that on those devices where you have set up caching, you have access to your information even if you are not connected to the internet. This caching application, of course, needs to maintain the same level of security and encryption as any password manager.

The caching application, along with a smartphone application, is something that they should make available but not require you to use in order for their product to be useful. It should be designed to increase the convenience of using the application without compromising the security. If a password manager application requires a locally installed application for the basic functions, then it is a local application with an online sync function, not an actual online manager.

One of the benefits of using an online application is that it doesn't require you to install anything. Another advantage is that there is little need for configuration, and this is beneficial for inexperienced users. With an online application, you just visit the website, log in, and you are ready to start using it. Depending on how sophisticated the tool is, you may have configuration options and settings that you can set at your leisure if you are so inclined, such as 2FA. Having basic and advanced settings is a great way to cater for both inexperienced and experienced users.

Online password managers often offer a browser plugin that allows for automatic saving of new account information as well as auto-filling websites with existing information. This is a great feature for phishing protection, which is something I'll cover later. In short, the auto-fill feature will only work on the same site that it was initially saved on, so if you find yourself on a different website, the autofill won't work.

For any reputable password manager, I would expect certain features:

- Strong data encryption, ideally using at least AES 256-bit level of encryption or stronger.

- Multifactor authentication (MFA). If they don't offer true multifactor authentication as I discussed before, be very afraid. The best options provide different choices of multifactor authentication, including multiple authenticator apps, and physical devices like FIDO U2F- or FIDO2-certified devices. As mentioned before, this is something a local password manager does not offer

- Ongoing monitoring of their solution, looking for issues that might compromise either security, integrity, or availability. This could manifest in several ways, including:

    o Server hard drive failure

    o Failure of the actual server

    o Connectivity failure

- o Configuration errors allowing unprivileged access

- o An intruder attempting to gain unauthorized access

- Robust controls and processes to prevent these issues from happening, quickly responding, and remediating when they do.

- Geo-distributed facilities. This means that they have multiple locations that are far from each other. So if there is an issue with one area, there are other locations that can pick up the load. An example of this would be separating the areas by time zones, for example, one in Seattle, WA, one in Denver, CO, one in Ashburn, VA, and one in Miami, FL. This way, if Seattle disappears due to an earthquake or volcano, then people outside Seattle can still access their data. If a hurricane wipes out Miami at the same time, people in unaffected regions can still access their data through the Denver and Ashburn locations. Which location your data is accessed in should be completely automated and transparent. If a company has multiple locations but your information is only stored at the location closest to where you signed up, then they do not offer geo-redundancy; they are merely optimizing for latency, assuming people never move.

- Frequent auditing and testing of security, procedures, and policies.

- A smartphone application for both Android and iPhone that maintains the same level of protection as the online app.

- A caching application that you can install on either macOS or Windows, either as a browser extension or as a separate application.

Some people would argue that online password managers are inherently less secure than a local password manager such as KeePass. They are very passionate in claiming that KeePass is the only way to go when it comes to password managers. I totally understand where they are coming from, but I feel that there is a flaw in their logic. Some of the fallacies include:

- They assume that one size fits all—that everyone's threat model is the same. I argue that no two threat models are the same.

- KeePass doesn't offer the MFA option that online password managers do.

- They feel that the mere fact of being online makes you less secure. Please refer back to my chapter on the balancing act. Yes, there are risks associated with being online, but if you handle them correctly, they are manageable. Just assuming that there is lower security is a fallacy.

  o Do you have the same rigor as an online provider in ensuring your computer isn't getting compromised?

o   If you are totally secure because your computer isn't connected to anything, why do you need a password manager?

o   Would you know if a hacker broke into your computer and stole your password file?

o   Do you upload your password manager database file to an online backup service or utilize an online file service such as Dropbox, iCloud, Box, Drive, or OneDrive? If so, how would you know if a criminal was able to get a copy of your database from one of those sources?

Yes, it is possible for an advanced user to further secure their local password manager; however, that may not apply to basic users. In the end, it comes down to a feeling of trust. If you have the skillset to set up and tweak your security in this manner, chances are you are not reading this book.

It is my expert opinion, based on the factors listed above, that a secure and well-respected online password manager is the best option for the basic user. Is it guaranteed to be 100 percent secure? Of course not—nothing is. As I outlined above, KeePass has risks; they are just different risks. When you consider all of the factors, I believe that online password managers are the safest option.

In fact, this is how I personally manage my passwords. I have been using a product called LastPass for many years. You can visit LastPass here (https://www.lastpass.com/). Their website has a lot of information about how it works and the features they offer. You can read about their approach to security at this link (https://lastpass.com/support_security.php) and here (https://www.lastpass.com/enterprise/security).

For the record, I highly recommend and endorse LastPass as a password manager. Everyone I know who is serious about properly managing their account information uses LastPass. I receive no kickback for that recommendation. Another popular online password manager is 1Password (https://1password.com/). I have no experience with it, nor do I know much about it. I have heard of people who are very happy with it in my circle, though LastPass is the most popular password manager.

Federated Logins

Another concept I want to cover under the topic of authentication is a concept known as *federated authentication* or *federated logins*. The term *federated* in this case has the same meaning as it does in everyday English. It is an adjective from the noun *federation*, meaning an organization or group where smaller divisions have some degree of internal autonomy.

What I am talking about here is when one site allows you to log in through another site. You see this most often with sites that are federated with Facebook, Google, Microsoft, and sometimes all three. So if you're on some blog site or another cool site, you authenticate to it by simply linking it to your Facebook account. This is convenient, as you don't have to manage another account and you can just log into this site with your Facebook account. Even better if you already have Facebook open and logged in; when you click on that Facebook icon on their login screen, you are instantly logged in.

Now I want to remind you of the discussion we had about the balancing act and how convenience can come at the cost of security. There is no denying that this is a very convenient option. Something to consider:

- When a site offers multiple federations, you need to track which one you used. I've ended up with multiple accounts on a website because I forgot which federations I used. Not a big deal, I know, but this can be confusing, especially if it is a subscription site and now it is bugging you to subscribe when you already did.

- Compromise of the federated site. For example, if your Facebook login is compromised, now all the sites that you federated with your Facebook login are compromised as well.

- Also, if the website, such as a blog, where you used the federated login is compromised, it is possible to leverage this on other sites.

My recommendation is to create a separate account with its own password rather than use federation.

Since I manage everything in my password manager, adding an extra account is no additional burden.

Remember Me

Another popular and convenient option is the *remember me, remember this computer*, or *stay logged in* prompts on website login screens. This is convenient, as you no longer need to log in again on that particular computer. What this means, though, is that if anyone can access your computer, they have the same convenient access as you do. You should rely heavily on your threat model when deciding if you should check that checkbox or not. The main thing to consider is what the chances are that your adversaries can get hold of that computer and end up with unrestricted access to your accounts.

How I deal with this is by never checking this prompt on any of my laptops, as I feel that it is possible that I might misplace one and not realize it for some time. On my cell phone, I often check this prompt, simply because the convenience factor is higher for me there and I feel I can keep my phone secured (it never leaves my side). On my desktop, which is physically secure in my home office, I have a greater tendency to check this, except on the most critical sites, like banking.

NSA, SSL, TLS, VPN, and TLA

In this section, I'm going to cover a lot of technical terms and various TLAs. As promised, I'll do my best to explain all the technical terms in a way that doesn't require computer expertise to understand. I should start by explaining what a TLA is. TLA stands for Three Letter Acronym, so a TLA is a TLA. There is nothing complicated to grasp here, just geeks trying to be funny about their acronyms. I will cover a whole slew of TLAs in this section, so let's get started.

NSA

In the context of this book, NSA is a TLA that stands for Network Security Architecture. As I mentioned before, I include it here as an example of TLA confusion; the same TLA can have multiple meanings. I did not include NSA here because I felt that basic online security needed to cover Network Security Architecture, as this is a concept that the IT department of a company always manages. Basically, NSA refers to how the company connects all its computers together to maximize its security.

SSL and TLS

In the section on encryption, I talked about secure vs. insecure connections. Let's now define the TLAs SSL and TLS. In short, these are methods of achieving a secure connection. SSL stands for Secure Socket Layer, the socket being the endpoint where the connection was terminated, like a mail stop or mailbox number. SSL was the original protocol used for securing the connection between a web browser on your computer and the web server that is serving your content. A new protocol, Transport Layer Security (TLS), has now replaced SSLs. There were several revisions of the SSL protocol. In the end, it was decided that the entire protocol had too many issues to live up to its security purpose. The protocol was initially invented by a company called Netscape Communications in 1994.

In 1999, the Internet Engineering Task Force (IETF) went back to the drawing board and drafted a new protocol based on SSL and called it Transport Layer Security (TLS). Securing specific sockets was no longer the mission; the whole transport layer needed to be secured, hence the rebranding. SSL was initially created specifically for securing web traffic. Now TLS is used for a lot more than that. Some people still use the SSL name even when talking about TLS, which can cause confusion.

For example, TLS version 1.0 is sometimes called SSL version 3.1. If this is all too confusing for you, don't worry too much about it. The critical thing to know is that TLS and SSL are methods (protocols) to secure your connection: SSL = old; TLS = new and improved. If you want to sound like you know what you are talking about with a techie who is talking about how their site is secured with SSL, ask them what version of SSL they are using. If they say anything lower than 3.1, ask them why they are using an old and outdated protocol instead of the new TLS protocol. That is, of course, assuming they don't respond with "TLS 1.0" or something along those lines.

Both TLS and SSL utilize asynchronous encryption to ensure the connection between your browser and the web server is secure. The little lock in your browser shows up to indicate that a secure connection has been established. If the lock is red, has a strike through it, or appears as an open lock, then you do not have a secure connection. Please bear in mind that TLS and SSL only secure your connection. They do not ensure that the web server is safe and do not mean that the network the web server is on is secure, only that your connection to the server is secure.

If we go back to the example of the miniature safes, the safe only guarantees that the content will get to its destination in a secure manner. Once the safe has been opened and the content removed, you have no control over what happens. Therefore, it is essential for you to figure out if you can trust the company running the web server. The fact that they set up a secure web server does not imply anything about their trust level. On the flip side, I would argue that any company that doesn't bother to at least do the minimal security and secure their web servers cannot be trusted. In the grand scheme of setting up a web server, enabling that level of security is fairly simple.

Also, your threat model will have to dictate whether having a secure connection to the web server is important. As with the postal mail example, considering the millions of envelopes they handle every hour of every day, what are the chances they'll pick your letter to read? It's the same if you are using an unsecured connection. The chance that anyone who has the opportunity to pick up your packet will actually pick up your packet is extremely slim.

Like I said, if the company can't even do the bare minimum of work and secure its web servers, it probably hasn't done any other security preparation. So I am very wary of any site that does not offer TLS protection—not because I'm worried about the connection being snooped on, but because I worry about how they'll manage any information I give them.

By the way, for those who are curious about the Netscape Communications Corporation, they created the very first internet browser, called Netscape Navigator, in 1994. A company called AOL, which was a huge internet provider in the 1990s, purchased Netscape Communications in 1999. The developers of Netscape split off and started the Firefox browser. After going through a lot of difficulties, including a failed merger with Time Warner in 2015, Verizon purchased AOL for $4.4 billion.

VPNs Defined

Let's get back on topic. Where was I again? Oh yes, TLAs. The next TLA I need to talk about is the concept of a VPN. VPN stands for Virtual Private Network. As I mentioned before, a network is just a technical term for connecting two or more computers together. A private network is when you connect those computers together in a private way. This means that nothing or no one on the outside of those computers can spy on what happens inside.

When you have a private network, only the computers involved in the private network can talk to each other, and all the connections are direct and isolated from all other connections.

In contrast, the internet is a public network, where everyone can talk to everyone, and the chances of being snooped on are high. So, what exactly is a virtual private network? This is a way that you can establish a private connection while utilizing public connections, so it is only virtually private, not physically private. The great thing about a VPN is that you can quickly turn it on and off. With a physically private network, if you want one of the computers to talk with computers outside the private network, you must unplug it from the private network and plug it into the other network, which can be a huge hassle.

A VPN is accomplished through an application you install on your computer. This software creates a secure connection to a designated VPN server. This secure connection can happen through either synchronous or asynchronous encryption, typically using TLS, with the key usually being a username/password combination. The detail of what encryption is used is an advanced topic beyond the scope of this book. You just need to know that VPN software will enable you to establish a virtual connection to a VPN server someplace else. This is often referred to as a *secure tunnel*.

Once this connection is established, all traffic from your computer will go through this connection and come out at the other end. All anyone will see is the tunnel; they can't see into the tunnel. If you are visiting TLS-enabled sites and you validate that the TLS connection is good, no one can see what you are browsing, but they can see which websites and web pages you are going to. If you have a VPN established, all they can see is that you have a VPN tunnel established. Here is the interesting part: The sites you are visiting will think you are the VPN server. The websites you are visiting have no idea where you are actually coming from, unlike when you're not using a VPN.

VPN Use Cases

I'm sure some of you have already spotted a strong case for using a VPN. That's privacy. Since no one can see what is in your tunnel, you have privacy from your network provider. Others on the internet, including your internet provider, cannot know any info about what sites you are visiting. Furthermore, since the sites see you as the VPN server, you also have location privacy.

So, what if you are physically located in, say, Germany and you have a VPN connection to a server in Dallas, TX. Where will the sites you are connecting to think you are physically located? In Dallas, TX, right? What benefits and drawbacks might come with that? I'll leave the answer to that as a thought exercise for you, the reader.

In addition to the privacy scenario, there is also a security benefit to using a VPN. If you don't know who is managing the network connection, or you don't trust them, you shouldn't connect, or you can establish a VPN connection immediately upon connecting. Using a VPN in this scenario will give you an encrypted tunnel into a network you can trust. An excellent example is public wireless hotspots, also known as public Wi-Fi. These are the restaurants, coffee houses, and other public places that offer free wireless internet. Even if they charge for it, that doesn't mean you can trust the service. Whenever you connect to one of these networks, having a VPN to provide that extra layer of security is highly recommended.

Problems with Public Hotspots

Hotspots are a garden variety privacy issue. The network operator might be monitoring everything you are doing. Even if you are using a secure TLS connection, the network operator can still see each connection; they just can't see the contents of the connection. For example, say you are browsing your favorite news site. The network operator cannot see which articles you called up, but they know which website you went to and how many articles you looked at. What they are actually looking at is the complete URL used for every article.

The bigger issue is the Man in the Middle (MiM) problem. This is where a criminal has control over the network you are connecting to and manipulates your traffic. The network could have been set up by someone with loose morals, or a criminal might have been able to seize control of the network after it was set up. It is also possible for a criminal to go to a public place with one of the portable hotspot devices that you can buy from any cellular carrier. They configure it to look like the actual public hotspot and entice nearby users to connect to their hotspot instead of the one managed by whatever public place you are in. Better yet, they go to a place that doesn't offer free wireless internet and pretend they are offering it on behalf of the business.

Regardless of how they came to control the network you are on, they own it and your connections. They can configure the network to use their laptop as something called a proxy server. A proxy server is basically a server that all traffic goes through for inspection or security and to proxy your connection in the normal sense of the word. In this configuration, all traffic goes through the laptop and is inspected there.

All TLS and SSL connections go through what is called SSL stripping. During SSL stripping, the criminal's laptop sees that you are trying to make an SSL connection. Rather than just letting it through as it would usually, it holds on to your connection request, then makes the same connection request itself. Then when the website responds, the criminal laptop copies everything it receives from the website and sends that to you in response to your connection request. This, of course, means that the criminal has an exact copy of everything that you are doing, including your usernames and passwords.

In most cases, you can tell that this is going on if you are paying attention to the lock in the browser, as it is not going to look right. In most cases, there won't be a lock at all, and the HTTPS in the address bar will change to HTTP (with the S missing). When you have an SSL or TLS connection in your browser, the address bar will always start with HTTPS. In this scenario, the VPN will most likely fail, which is a clue to you that something is not right. If you have a secure VPN connection, you can be assured that no one is snooping on your connection.

Selecting a Good VPN Service

If you are looking at all the different VPN services out there, make sure you stay away from the free offerings. If you need a VPN, spending money on it is worth it and helps to ensure that the provider is legit. A free VPN service is likely to be just a Man in the Middle (MiM) trap. Keep in mind that a VPN only protects you as far as the VPN server. You are, in a way, just moving the trust boundary. Establishing a VPN tunnel because you don't trust your internet provider when you know even less about the VPN provider is not a smart approach.

So you must make sure you can trust your VPN provider. If you are a mobile worker, your employer will provide you with a VPN service if that is important to them. In this case, just use what they give you for all work functions and don't worry about it. For personal things, it comes down to company policies on using company equipment for personal business, as well as how your employer fits into your threat model.

For a VPN for personal use, you're going to have to do some research. You can read online reviews and read up on each provider. Hopefully, the knowledge you gain from this book will help you discern the good from the bad. Some of the things to look for are:

- Their privacy statement—read it carefully.

- o Do they sound believable?

- o Are they coherent and free of inconsistencies?

- How much do they want to know about you?

  - o Do they want to know your name, e-mail, and phone number? A great VPN provider doesn't ask questions.

- Do they keep any traffic logs?

- What payment methods do they offer?

- Do they only offer PayPal and credit card options?

- Or do they offer gift cards and other anonymized payment methods?

- Who owns the company running the VPN service and what country are they located in?

The reason it is important that they don't ask any personal questions is because that indicates they care about your privacy. There is no reason why a VPN provider needs to know your name or e-mail. If they don't have any information about you, then they can't sell your information.

Personally, I use a service called Private Internet Access, which you can visit at this link (https://www.privateinternetaccess.com/).

The company that owns ProtonMail also offers a VPN service called ProtonVPN. This would be another excellent choice for a VPN service. I do not, however, use them because of a policy issue I have with them. They have a policy that if you are using Slack, Skype, Instant Messenger, or other similar communication services, you are not allowed to use their auto-connect feature. I do not know if Facebook falls into the same group or not, as I never log into Facebook. You are required to do a manual configuration where you specifically choose to connect only to what they call their peer-to-peer servers.

They will periodically disconnect your session if you are connected to their regular servers and have Slack, Skype, or similar programs running in the background. Private Internet Access is just as good, and they don't care if you are using those applications. So it is much easier to use them, and that is why I use them instead of ProtonVPN. If you do not use any chat, social media, or other similar communication service, then ProtonVPN might be a good option for you; otherwise, I recommend you check out Private Internet Access.

Malware Threats

The term *malware* is a contraction of *malicious software*. The malware category is vast, and many books have been written on that topic alone. For the purposes of this book, a basic awareness of malware, the danger it poses, and how one might get infected by malware is enough. Spoiler alert: The leading cause is clicking on links and opening attachments.

Viruses and Worms

These are the oldest malware types out there; chances are good that you've heard of these and you may even have experienced them. These are self-propagating and do damaging things to your computer, kind of like how a human virus impacts the human body.

Trojan Horse

This category of malware was inspired by the Trojan horse from Greek mythology. The story recounts how the Greeks invaded the city of Troy (modern Hissarlik, Turkey) somewhere between 1100 and 1300 BC. According to the story, after a long battle for the city of Troy where the Greeks were unable to make any advances, the Greek army built this huge wooden horse on wheels and left it for the citizens of Troy as a parting gift. The people of Troy were very appreciative of this sweet gesture and rolled the horse into town. The only problem was that the Greek army was hiding inside of it. The Greek army made a surprise exit from the wooden horse and destroyed the city of Troy.

A malware Trojan horse operates in a very similar fashion. A malicious application will masquerade as something interesting or useful, and it is often free. Over the years these have come in many forms, but animated birthday cards have often been a popular choice. Literally any of those applications out there on the internet could be Trojan malware. While you are playing music or watching some cute animation or something, the real application is doing its thing in the background. Just like a Trojan can masquerade as any application, it can hide any type of malware.

The following threats exist with or without a Trojan.

- Remote Access Trojans (RATs) will install software on your computer that will allow the threat actor to control your computer remotely in order to do its bidding. This can include anything from stealing files from your computer to performing criminal acts from your computers.

  - Your computer can become part of something known as a botnet. A botnet is a network of compromised computers that a threat actor can remotely and automatically control to hack or take down networks en masse or perform a mass compromise operation.

  - I have heard stories of people getting arrested on federal felony charges based on evidence that led to their computer. If I recall correctly, they were set free after investigators found a RAT on their computer.

- People have lost their jobs when a breach of company data was traced back to their workstation due to a RAT infection.

  - If you realize that you did something you shouldn't have and it could have infected you with malware, immediately inform your IT department so that they can clean it up.

  - Trying to hide it will only make things worse for you.

  - Kind of like what we teach our kids:

    - Owning up to your mistakes may or may not get you punished.

    - Trying to hide a mistake and lying about it will get you punished for hiding it.

- Ransomware is where the malicious application will actually encrypt all of the data on your computer. When you try to access any files, you get a ransom demand. These have been known to come as Trojans, worms, and just plain malware. A ransomware worm will not stop at just encrypting your computer; it will find other computers connected to yours and encrypt them as well.

o   A *keylogger* or *spyware* is malware that is specifically designed to spy on you. It will capture all of your keystrokes, including usernames, passwords, and credit card numbers, and monitor what applications you use and what websites you visit. Some even capture videos with your webcam. The result of the spying is uploaded to the threat actor's computer for them to profit from in any number of ways.

o   Destructive malware will just delete files from your hard drive purely to be destructive. The author of this type of malware is just a plain and simple vandal. Typically, they don't just place them in the trash bin where you can retrieve them from. They do what is called a *secure erase*. A secure erase is defined in the privacy section earlier. It makes the files irrecoverable.

o   Annoyance or adware malware operators will just get their kicks out of annoying the crap out of you. They'll change your background, give you unexpected pop-ups, play random sounds at random times, and randomly open advertisement sites. All of these things can drive you crazy, but they have no direct destructive or harmful intent. These are often motivated to gain fake views on an advertising page. By having more users visiting their site, they can charge advertisers more. There is the possibility that adware malware could load an ad that happens to be loaded with different malware, so there is that to consider.

Malvertising

Malvertising is when you have online advertisements laced with malware. According to the Center for Internet Security (CIS), this is a big problem on the rise that is hard to combat. To combat this problem, I simply use an ad blocker in my browser. If the ads never load, they can't infect you. This will degrade your online experience, as sites that depend on ad revenue will whine about your ad blocker and try to convince you to disable the ad blocker just for them. If you give in to all of them, eventually your ad blocker will be useless. Some sites may block you from their content if you have an ad blocker enabled. This is a perfect time to engage your critical thinking skills and decide whether the risk of malware outweighs your desire to access certain sites. Here is a partial screen capture of one such complaint:

Do your part to support us

9 out of 10 people don't use adblock on our site.

Figure 21: Adblocker complaint

Their claim that nine out of ten people don't use an adblocker is a very weak argument. It is similar to the argument that nine out of ten people smoke cigarettes, therefore you should smoke as well. Their argument tells me that nine out of ten people do not understand the danger of malvertising. Rather than complaining about the ad blockers, the site owners should be reassuring their users that their site is free from malvertising and clarifying the steps they have taken to ensure their security. Offering a subscription alternative might be another option for them. Anyway, I digress again.

Ways to Get Infected with Malware

- The most common way to get infected with malware is by opening unexpected attachments or clicking on unexpected links.

- Another way is by clicking on unsavory links on questionable sites.

- The second most common way is via USB devices.

  - Random USB devices. If you find a USB drive in the parking lot or some public place that has some enticing label like Top Secret or My Pictures, leave it alone, because it is probably laced with malware. Same goes for finding a random mouse or any other device just lying around in a public place. Even if it doesn't look like a drive, it could have a drive hidden in it that could infect your computer with malware the moment you plug it in.

o   Bulk bins at your local retailer with USB devices that have no packages are dangerous. A threat actor could hide malware on these devices without anyone knowing it. Is the discount on the device worth the risk of getting a malware infection? Even if they have packaging, if the packaging isn't tamper-proof, be very cautious. This is referred to as a supply chain problem in information security circles. This is when a threat actor is able to tamper with your equipment before you even purchase it. This isn't a huge problem for the average consumer, but it's been known to happen. You can reduce your risk by only buying things in tamper-proof packaging, only buying things that are behind the counter, or buying them from a reputable online store. Buying used USB devices online or buying from unknown merchants on sites like Craigslist, eBay, Alibaba, and Amazon carry the same risk factor. As with everything in cybersecurity, there are no guarantees. The supply chain problem runs deep. Just like a chain has many links in it, so does a supply chain. Messing with things in a retail store that are out in the open is the easiest, but that doesn't stop a criminal from infecting products at the distribution point or at the manufacturer's site. Again, not a huge concern for consumers, just something to be aware of.

- o Public smartphone charging stations. Picture this: You carry around a smartphone—after all, who doesn't carry power-hungry smartphones these days? —and the battery is about to die. You see a charging station at the mall, at the stadium, or wherever you are. You think, "I'm safe. I can charge my phone and continue to use it." Be very careful of those stations; while most of those are legit, some are known as malware watering holes. While your phone is charging, all the data is being copied off your phone, and it is now infected with nasty malware. Your best defense here is abstinence, but if you must indulge, use protection where possible. You can find data blockers online; for example, searching Amazon for "charging data blocker" provides several options. This only works if you carry your own cable and plug into a regular USB port. If the charging station provides the cable, I have not found any protection for that. The best way to abstain is to carry your own charger and just find an outlet. An even better option is to carry a power bank. A power bank is a portable charger that has an internal battery and that can charge your phone without being plugged in. Here are a few examples of power banks: (https://www.anker.com/products/1 07/power-banks). I own several dozen power banks from Anker, as well as some of their other products, and I love them all. Anker customer support is legendary as well.

Protection Approaches

Now, how do you protect yourself against these threats?

- Don't click on links you don't know (I may have mentioned this one before). More details on this in the section on phishing.

- Don't visit questionable sites, even if they claim to offer free videos of pussy cats, dogs or other enticing videos. Stick to well-known and reputable sites.

- If you receive an e-mail or someone tells you about this great site offering pirated movies or videos, just delete and ignore it. Also:

- o If you enter the site, you'll probably get malware.

- o Downloading pirated movies makes you an accomplice to electronic piracy.

- o Electronic piracy is a federal crime under title 17 of the United States Code.

  - Per 17 US Code 1204 section A: Punishable by up to five years in jail and fines of up to $500,000 for a first offense, twice that for a repeat offense.

  - Most serious criminal cases are considered federal felonies. Is avoiding paying 20 dollars for that movie worth being a convicted felon?

- o Most importantly, it is immoral and wrong. Respect the artist enough to pay for their work.

- Don't open attachments in unexpected e-mails. Unless you are expecting an attachment from a source you trust, don't open it without validating what it is with the person who sent it. If you don't know the person who sent it, don't open it or click on any links in the e-mail under any circumstances. If you get an unexpected e-mail from DHL that instructs you to open an attachment to learn the status of your shipment, don't open it, as it is malware.

Example

Here is a screenshot of a sample malware e-mail claiming to be from DHL. Notice the "From" address. The attachment is undoubtedly malware.

Received: Friday, February 1, 2019 9:23 AM

From: DHL EXPRESS Florian@antiquesofperkasie.com

To:

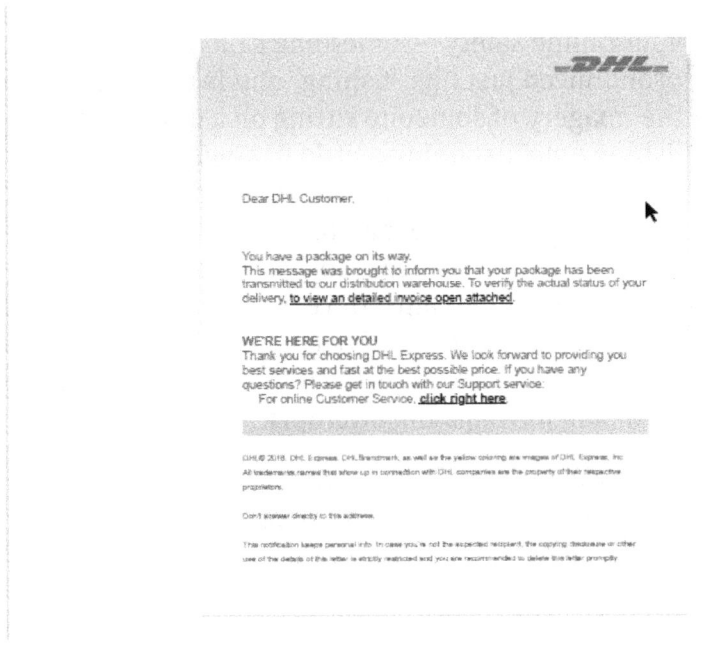

Dear DHL Customer,

You have a package on its way.
This message was brought to inform you that your package has been transmitted to our distribution warehouse. To verify the actual status of your delivery, **to view an detailed invoice open attached.**

WE'RE HERE FOR YOU
Thank you for choosing DHL Express. We look forward to providing you best services and fast at the best possible price. If you have any questions? Please get in touch with our Support service.
For online Customer Service, **click right here.**

DHL© 2018, DHL, Express, DHL Brandmark, as well as the yellow coloring are images of DHL Express, Inc. All trademarks named that show up in connection with DHL companies are the property of their respective proprietors.

Don't answer directly to this address.

This notification keeps personal info. In case you're not the expected recipient, the copying disclosure or other use of the details of this letter is strictly restricted and you are recommended to delete this letter promptly.

rgent notice.doc
44.57 KB

Figure 22: DHL malware e-mail example

Scams, Cons, and Other Dangers

In this section, I want to discuss the topic of scams, frauds, and other dangers. These things may or may not be a direct security threat. These items could be a threat to your wallet or just merely a waste of time. A lot of people already know about some of these topics, but I feel it is important to cover them anyway for the sake of comprehensive coverage.

Let's Go Phishing

In this chapter, I'll cover one of the biggest threats to your online safety—something called *phishing*. It is pronounced just like "fishing" and is meant to evoke the imagery of someone sitting on a dock with their fishing pole just doing a little fishing. Except in this imagery the fisherman is a threat actor and you are the fish, and the threat actor is trying to get someone on the hook, so to speak. So, yes, phishing is all about fraud and scams. Here is a little spoiler for you in terms of how to avoid becoming a phishing victim. If you don't click on stuff that you don't know, you won't fall for phishing attempts.

What the threat actor is trying to phish for varies. Sometimes they are just after your money, and the goal is to get money from you. Other times they are after information that they can benefit from. For example, instead of getting you to give them some small sum of money, they trick you into giving them your bank login. That way, they can log into your bank and take whatever money they want, whenever they want, so they do not need to contact you anymore.

This is one of the most prevalent phishing attacks out there. Another widespread phishing attack tricks you into providing your work account info or installing malware on your work computer so the criminal can get access to your work environment. These types of phishing attack are limitless; they all have a common theme. They are trying to get you to do something you shouldn't or give them information you aren't supposed to give out.

Phishing is often done as a large campaign, where thousands or even hundreds of thousands of users are targeted, casting a wide net, so to speak. Other times it is very specific, sometimes even targeting a particular person; these are referred to as spear phishing, whaling, or CEO fraud, depending on who is being targeted.

Phishing also happens over various media.

- When phishing happens over the phone, it is called *vishing*, which is a contraction of voice phishing.

- When phishing happens over text messaging, it is called *SMiShing*. That is a contraction of SMS and phishing, SMS being the technical name for text messages. SMS stands for Short Message Service. The name refers to its origin, when text messages were limited in length, similar to Twitter messages. The original limit for text messages was 160 characters. Modern versions have implemented concatenation into the protocol, so modern phones automatically split your long text messages into smaller chunks. This makes it so that the messages fit into the 160-character limit, and it can be auto-assembled at the other end.

- E-mail phishing is just plain phishing, no cute contraction. Maybe no one could think of a fun contraction for e-mail phishing. Eshing just doesn't have the same ring to it, I guess.

Regardless of how targeted the campaign is or what communication medium the criminals use, they are all the same scam, relying heavily on social engineering. Phishing attacks follow a very predictable formula, but it varies how cleverly and skillfully the formula is implemented.

When it comes to a phishing attack, there is always an urgent need to act right away. If they are clever, they will invoke fear, guilt, greed, or some other strong emotion. They want to trick you into acting without thinking, and they will often try to get you emotional so you are less likely to be logical. They want to provoke you into action. What that action may be depends on the delivery platform and their end goal.

If this happens over e-mail and they want to infect and take over your computer, there will often be an attachment you have to click on right now or the whole world is going to implode. Of course, that attachment is a virus that will wreak havoc on your computer. Often with e-mail phishing they will get you to click on a link that might download a virus or take you to a form to collect information from you, or both. The information they try to collect is usually private or personally identifiable information that they can leverage to make money. In the banking fraud example, they'll construct a form that looks like the bank login page so that they can collect your bank login information. I will provide some examples in a bit.

If it is over text messaging, they will either get you to click a link or text back some information. Most often it is a link. It seems that most of the SMiShing messages I've received lately call me Desiree—not sure why, but it is sloppy and makes it easy to spot. They are usually tempting me with free money or an easy work from home opportunity with great pay—in other words, also free money.

If it is via a phone call, they are usually after information or money. They want your bank information or credit card information. In some cases, they try to pressure you into giving them gift card numbers. In some of the ploys that I've heard, they claim to be your local police department or the US Federal Internal Revenue Service (IRS) letting you know that you have a huge fine outstanding, and if you don't pay it right now over the phone you will be arrested. I'm sure you all know this, but I'm going to say it anyway.

The police department, the IRS, or any other law enforcement agency will never call you up and demand money over the phone; it simply won't happen. If a law enforcement agency, for example, the police, IRS, or the FBI, has an urgent need to talk to you, regardless of the reason, they won't call. They will track you down and send a few officers to chat with you and, if needed, bring you in. So if the scenario ever came up where an outstanding fine warranted an arrest—which I find doubtful—the police wouldn't call first. They'd simply show up and take you to the station. If you had the option to pay the fine to avoid arrest, they'd escort you to the appropriate clerk's office and wait while you settled your debt in person. Here is a tweet from Bellevue WA Police on this topic: (https://twitter.com/BvuePD/status/11312825409 94555904/)

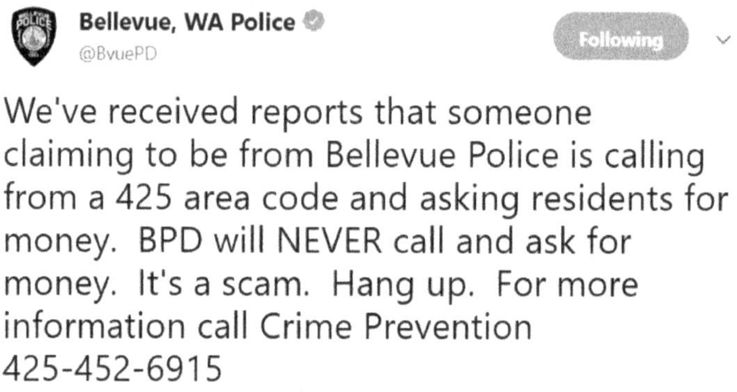

Bellevue, WA Police ✔
@BvuePD

Following ⌄

We've received reports that someone claiming to be from Bellevue Police is calling from a 425 area code and asking residents for money. BPD will NEVER call and ask for money. It's a scam. Hang up. For more information call Crime Prevention 425-452-6915

Figure 23: Bellevue PD scam warning

Also, here is one from Seattle WA Police that is a similar scam. (https://twitter.com/SeattlePD/status/115229070 1792571393)

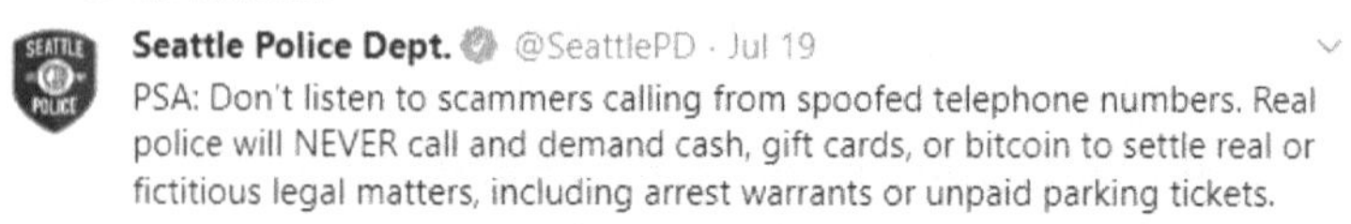

Seattle Police Dept. ✔ @SeattlePD · Jul 19

⌄

PSA: Don't listen to scammers calling from spoofed telephone numbers. Real police will NEVER call and demand cash, gift cards, or bitcoin to settle real or fictitious legal matters, including arrest warrants or unpaid parking tickets.

Figure 24: Seattle PD scam warning

Another popular vishing scheme is when they claim to be calling from either Microsoft or Apple to tell you that is there something wrong with your computer and they are going to fix it for you. I believe their end goal with this scam is to get you to install something that will supposedly help you but is in fact malware. They will also charge you for their "help." If you have ever had to call either of those companies, you know that getting them to call you back when you are actually paying them is hard enough. They will never call you unexpectedly like that.

For one thing, think about the privacy implications if they were able to tell that there was something wrong with your computer before you did. The liability associated with such a service that was thrust upon the computer owner without their knowledge or consent would be unimaginable, and thus simply won't happen.

One important thing to consider in this context is to make sure you know what companies and institutions you deal with. If there are things you have other people manage for you, let them know about any contact you get regarding that service. For example, I manage the website for a small business that a friend of mine owns. I told her that if she receives any e-mails, letters, or phone calls to do with her website, don't respond to them—let me know, and I will deal with it. All legitimate companies that deal with her website have me registered as a contact, so any contact she is receiving is because someone looked up the main contact information for her business for the purpose of scams.

For things you manage, like your banking, make sure you know what banks you do business with. If you bank with a local credit union and you get an e-mail talking about an issue with your Bank of America account, immediately consider it a scam.

Now that I've described the threat in some detail, let's talk about how to detect it and respond. The very first thing you need to do whenever you are online or get an unsolicited phone or text message is to engage your critical thinking skills and avoid getting emotional. If you feel you are getting riled up or emotional about something you are reading online, pull yourself back and analyze the situation. Think logically, think critically, and avoid getting emotional. To parody an old and tired cliché, if you let yourself get emotional, the criminal wins. If you think it might not be a scam, independently research any claims, and don't take anything at face value. Once you have independently verified the facts presented to you, then you can act on them, emotions and all.

This is a good time to touch on something called *disinformation campaigns*, otherwise known as propaganda campaigns. It has been reported by independent investigators that there is a high amount of propaganda going on in the US these days, especially when it comes to social media. I am sure the US is only one of many countries exposed to an extreme number of disinformation campaigns. The reports from these investigators state that foreign nation states are deliberately sowing discontent in the US, pitting US citizens against each other. If we are busy fighting, then we're not paying attention to what they are doing. This has influenced elections in the past.

Keep in mind that some of the disinformation campaigns waged against various societies are usually convincing, and they often create multiple fake sites to promote their propaganda. Therefore, sifting through the garbage can be challenging. Even reputable news outlets have been tricked into promoting what later turned out to be propaganda.

When you are enjoying your social media, it is crucial that you use your critical thinking skills and research everything you read online before accepting it as the truth. Many of the viral videos and messages that are emotionally charged is proven fake disinformation designed to spread hatred and discord throughout the US. Of course, adorable viral cat videos are excluded from this. I believe this is a prevalent issue for other countries as well.

Whatever you do, never click on strange links or open unknown attachments. If I'm repeating myself, it is because this is important, and it is essential that this idea sinks in. Repetition has been shown to help with assimilation. I'll probably mention this a few more times for emphasis. If you receive an e-mail claiming to be from your bank, promising financial doom if you don't click on their link right this second, and you are worried that it might be authentic, then contact your bank to confirm. Whatever you do, do not click on that link or open any attachment. Use the number in your phone book, call the number on the back of your bank card, or use the link saved in your bookmarks to contact your bank and investigate this claim. In other words, if you wanted to contact your bank without having this e-mail, use that method.

I'll say it again: If you want to validate the legitimacy of the e-mail, then contact your bank through your usual means—don't click on that link. Clicking on links in e-mails or opening unexpected attachments is the number one way to get yourself infected with something nasty that will completely ruin your day. Therefore, if online security and privacy are important to you, never click on links or open attachments in unexpected e-mails.

If the e-mail is from a bank you don't do business with and you worry that you have a bank account you forgot about, then Google the bank name for contact information and contact the bank to verify. Do not use any contact information in the e-mail and do not click on any links or open any attachments.

Have I mentioned about not clicking on any links or opening any attachments? Am I flogging a dead horse yet?

If you get a scam phone call, there are a few ways to manage it. Some people find it fun to toy with the criminal, to pretend they have you hooked and string them along. Others try to turn the tables on them and pretend that they are religious fanatics who want to convert them. The point of this approach is to keep them on the line so they can't scam someone more gullible. Me, I don't have time for that, so I hang up the moment I realize it's just another scam call.

It is because of the prevalence of scam calls that I don't even answer calls from numbers that I don't recognize anymore. If the number isn't in my phone book, I let it go to voicemail. If it is important, they'll leave a message and I can call them back. The only exception is if I'm expecting a call from an unknown number.

If the scam is coming through text messages, check with your provider to see if they have any procedures for dealing with spam messages. If not, just delete the message and move on with your life.

For an e-mail message, most of the popular e-mail clients now offer a "report phishing" option in their client. This actually sends that message to a group that collects and analyzes phishing messages. Those groups are trying to build software that can automatically detect and manage all phishing e-mails while not touching anything else. This is currently an elusive goal, but I believe it is a worthy endeavor, and I admire them for trying. Go ahead and use the phishing report feature in your e-mail client to make that phishing e-mail go away. Just don't click on anything in the e-mail.

Some phishing e-mails are easier to spot than others, so let's look at some of the examples I pulled out of my personal e-mail inbox. Here is one that is half decent:

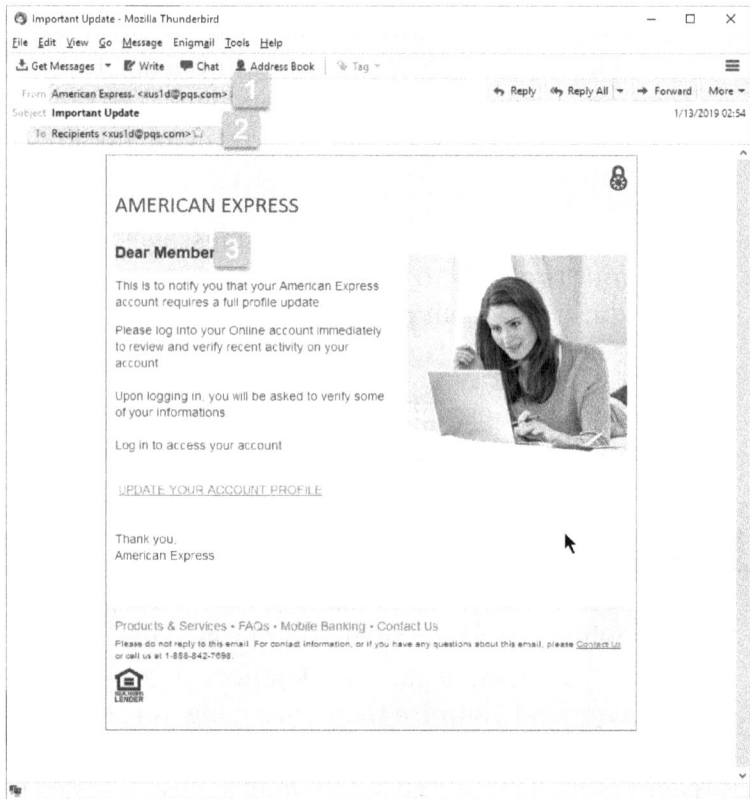

Figure 25: Phishing example 1: American Express

Multiple things jump out at me that say that this a
phishing e-mail. The very first thing is the fact that I
don't have an American Express card, which means I
don't have an account to update. The second thing is
more subjective, and it is the design. While the e-
mail looks very professional, it doesn't seem like a
design American Express would use. It feels more
like a canned design. Beyond those indicators, there
are at least three immediate red flags, which I
highlighted and numbered. The first red flag is that
that is not an American Express e-mail address.

This criminal was too lazy to spoof the "From" address, which is so simple and would have taken them an extra five minutes. The second red flag is that a financial institution always puts the customer's e-mail address in the "To" field. Again, this criminal was too lazy to send a custom e-mail, so they sent the e-mail to themselves and blind copied all the victims. Blind carbon copy (Bcc) is a technique available in all e-mail clients where you can specify multiple e-mail addresses without any of them seeing the other e-mails.

This is a somewhat controversial feature, as some people call it sneaky. The biggest benefit of this feature is privacy. The most legitimate scenario in which to use the Bcc feature is when you want to send an e-mail to all your friends who may not know each other, and they may not want their e-mail exposed to everyone. This feature should only be used for personal reasons, never by a corporation. Any marketing mail that uses this feature immediately loses credibility for me. You can immediately recognize that this feature was used because your e-mail address isn't on the To or CC line.

CC stands for Carbon Copy, and it is a way to include other people and indicate that they weren't the target audience; it's just keeping them in the loop. The third red flag is that e-mails from financial institutions will address you by name. In fact, any legitimate marketing e-mail will look like a flyer that might be included with your newspaper or something you might pick up in their stores, or it will be highly personalized. Any e-mail that starts with "Dear member," "Dear Sir," or "To whom it may concern" should be considered suspicious. Of course, an exception to that is if you are used to getting e-mails like that from a club or an organization you are a member of and this e-mail follows the pattern and style of previous e-mails.

Now here is an example where they put more effort into their scam and probably got a better return on their investment.

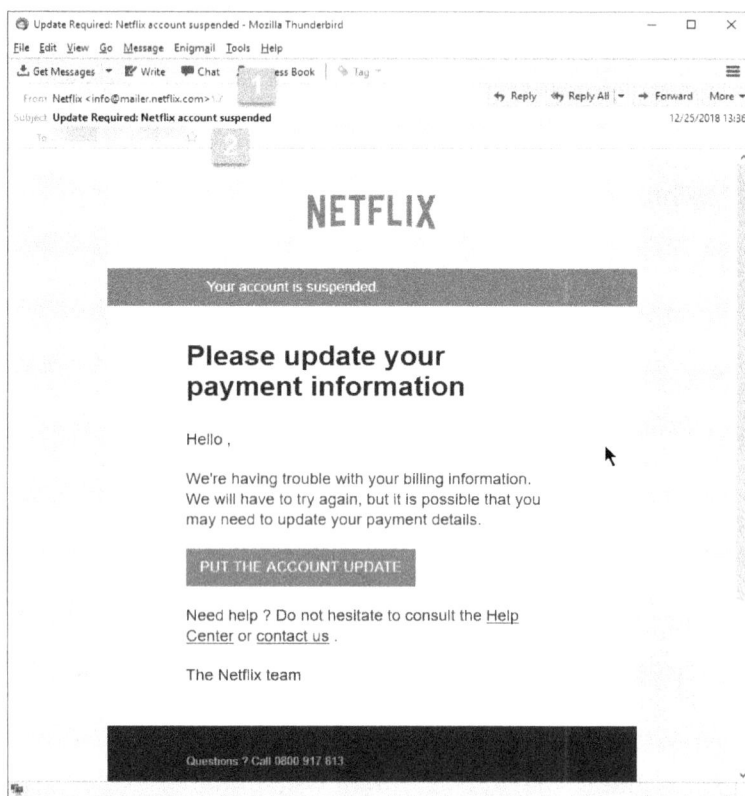

Figure 26: Phishing example 2: Netflix

To me, this looks like an e-mail I would expect to receive from Netflix. Notice the sense of urgency to click on a link, one of the hallmarks of a phishing attack.

1. Notice that they took the effort to spoof a "From" address that looks like an address Netflix might use.

2. Being the super geek I am, I have dozens of e-mail addresses, and this went to an e-mail account that Netflix doesn't have. For most of you, that isn't something you can use.

The only way I was able to positively tell that this was a phishing e-mail was through something called the hover detection. In all web browsers and e-mail clients, if you take your mouse and move it over a link and just leave it there, without clicking, the address behind that link will appear in the bottom of the screen. Let's look at an example.

Figure 27: Netflix phishing, hover demo 1

Here you can see me hovering over the help link in the e-mail. Look at the bottom of that image. Let's zoom in on that a little.

Figure 28: Netflix demo 1 hover zoom

Do you recognize the URL from our earlier discussion? In this e-mail, even though it is a phishing e-mail, the help link looks legit because the organization part of the URL is Netflix. Now let's do the same for the big red square they want you to click on.

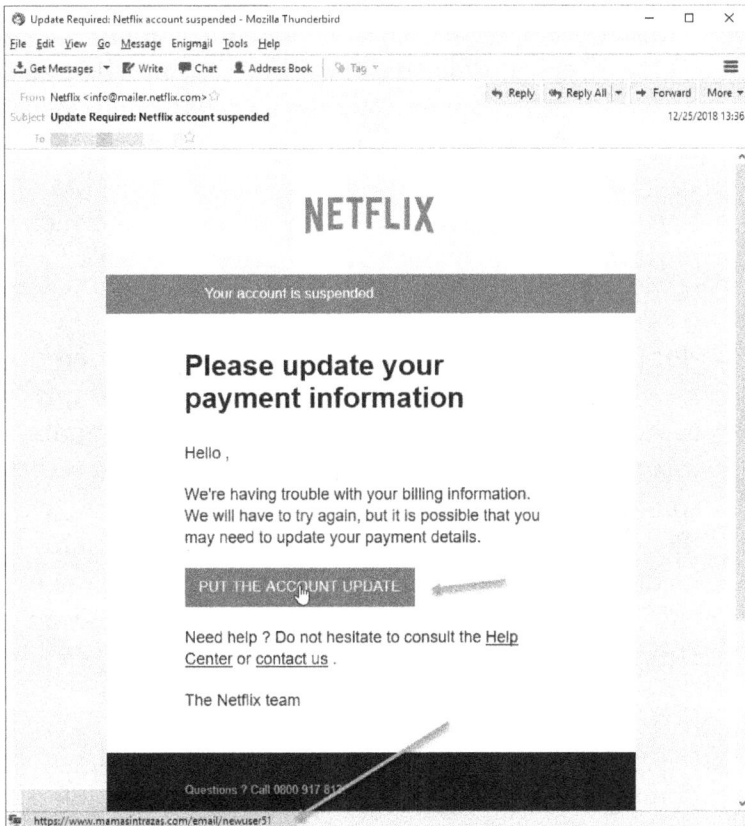

Figure 29: Netflix phishing, hover demo 2

Also, lets zoom in on the URL at the bottom there.

https://www.mamasintrazas.com/email/newuser51

Figure 30: Netflix phishing, hover demo 2, zoom

Notice any difference? Referring back to the earlier chapter on URLs, notice how the FQDN isn't from Netflix. Now, sophisticated criminals will make the URL look confusingly similar to the real Netflix URL without it being correct. Once you understand how a URL works from the chapter on URLs, you won't get fooled by https://www.apple.com.rusky.ru/. Others are harder to detect. For example, do you trust yourself to notice the difference between Netflix and Natflix? If you're not great at decoding URLs, which most inexperienced users aren't, then this isn't a foolproof method.

Not to worry; I have an absolutely foolproof method for you that I may have mentioned before—simply never click on links in e-mails or open attachments. It is really that simple. If you accidentally click on something while you were trying to hover, just close the window immediately before it has a chance to load. If you never click on anything and never open any attachment, whether the message is a phishing e-mail or not becomes irrelevant.

Now you may be asking yourself: what if Netflix really has suspended your account because of a billing problem? No problem. If you get an e-mail like that, just try to watch something on Netflix. Just make sure that you use your usual method to watch Netflix that does not include clicking on a link in an e-mail. If you can watch your favorite show as usual, you know the e-mail was a scam. If there is an issue with your membership billing, Netflix will point that out when you try to watch a show. They will tell you to fix that issue before you can watch your show. Apologies if I sound like a broken record; like I said, repeating critical information has been shown to help with retention. Furthermore, it is incredible how much you can improve your security simply by never clicking on anything in an e-mail.

The only time it is acceptable to click on a link in an e-mail or open an attachment is when you were expecting an e-mail with a link or an attachment, or you have verified that the e-mail came from a trusted source. Here are a few scenarios to illustrate this point.

- You are signing up to a news site that you feel has some great articles. During the sign-up process, they ask you for your e-mail address, and then they tell you to check your e-mail and find the e-mail they just sent you. They ask you to click on a link in that e-mail to prove that you own the e-mail address you gave them. This would fall under the expected e-mail category. Don't randomly click on links in any old e-mail; find the e-mail that looks like it came from that site in the last couple of minutes.

- You are on the phone with your friend, and you are planning a trip. She tells you that she is sending you an e-mail with some travel info in it. You check your e-mail, and sure enough, there is an e-mail that looks like it came from your friend with the travel information. This e-mail would be safe to open and it would be safe to click on the links. Now if you see an e-mail from your friend that does not appear to have anything to do with travel info, it would be prudent to ask your friend about that e-mail before you click on anything in it.

- You are going through your e-mail, and you come across an e-mail that looks like it came from your friend, but you weren't expecting anything, and it looks a little off. So you call your friend or send a text message asking about it. Your friend confirms that they sent it and gives you the back story. Now you've validated that the e-mail did indeed come from a trusted source. To be extra safe, don't reply to the suspicious e-mail. Reach out using any other means.

Now, keep in mind that there are multiple levels of trust. You can have a trusted source and have validated that the e-mail came from a trusted source, but you also know that person sends you sketchy files or links. This is where critical thinking comes into play, to analyze if it is worth the risk of opening it.

Here are some additional examples of e-mails that are attempting to scare you into doing something stupid, like clicking on a link in a random unexpected e-mail.

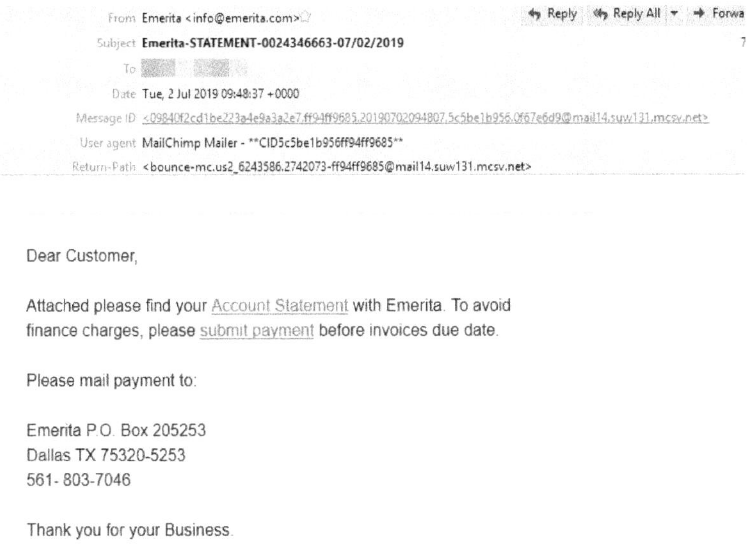

From Emerita <info@emerita.com> ↩ Reply ↩ Reply All ▾ → Forwa

Subject **Emerita-STATEMENT-0024346663-07/02/2019** 7

To

Date Tue, 2 Jul 2019 09:48:37 +0000

Message ID <0984012cd1be223a4e9a3a2e7.ff94ff9685.20190702094807.5c5be1b956.0f67e6d9@mail14.suw131.mcsv.net>

User agent MailChimp Mailer - **CID5c5be1b956ff94ff9685**

Return-Path <bounce-mc.us2_6243586.2742073-ff94ff9685@mail14.suw131.mcsv.net>

Dear Customer,

Attached please find your Account Statement with Emerita. To avoid finance charges, please submit payment before invoices due date.

Please mail payment to:

Emerita P.O. Box 205253
Dallas TX 75320-5253
561- 803-7046

Thank you for your Business.

Figure 31: Phishing example 1

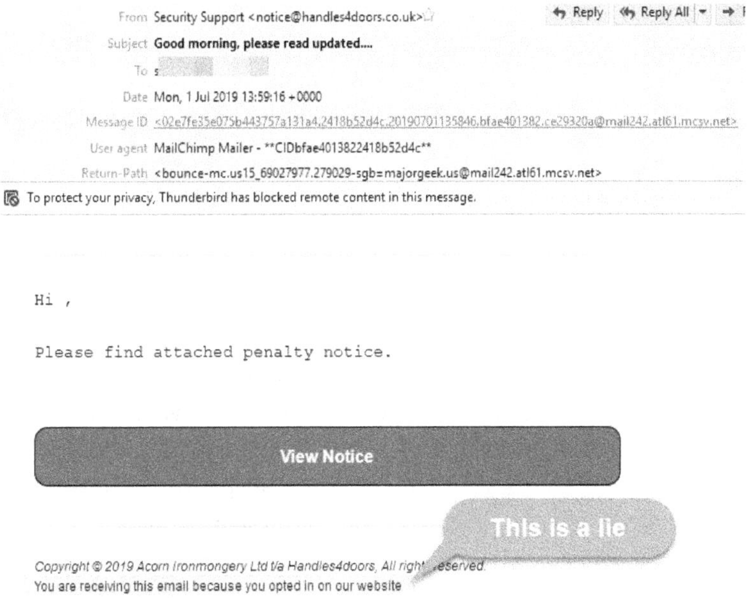

From Security Support <notice@handles4doors.co.uk> ↩ Reply ↩ Reply All ▾ → F

Subject **Good morning, please read updated....**

To s

Date Mon, 1 Jul 2019 13:59:16 +0000

Message ID <02e7fe35e075b443757a131a4.2418b52d4c.20190701135846.bfae401382.ce29320a@mail242.atl61.mcsv.net>

User agent MailChimp Mailer - **CIDbfae4013822418b52d4c**

Return-Path <bounce-mc.us15_69027977.279029-sgb=majorgeek.us@mail242.atl61.mcsv.net>

To protect your privacy, Thunderbird has blocked remote content in this message.

Hi ,

Please find attached penalty notice.

View Notice

This is a lie

Copyright © 2019 Acorn Ironmongery Ltd t/a Handles4doors, All right reserved.
You are receiving this email because you opted in on our website

Figure 32: Phishing example 2

From Law Notice <aristocratnews@aristocrat.com>   ↩ Reply   ↩ Reply All   ▾   → For
Subject **Notice # 545**
To
Date Mon, 1 Jul 2019 13:14:09 +0000
Message ID <34c2a0898d480b97c5d2202b2.f337bc0d5b.20190701131338.6a699e2f61.aada821d@mail33.suw111.mcdlv.net>
User agent MailChimp Mailer - **CID6a699e2f61f337bc0d5b**
Return-Path <bounce-mc.us6_12886459.808989-sgb=majorgeek.us@mail33.suw111.mcdlv.net>

🛡 To protect your privacy, Thunderbird has blocked remote content in this message.

Please find attached penalty notice regarding your order # 434555 made June 25 at 11:54 am.

Print Notice

Copyright © 2019 Aristocrat Technologies. All rights reserved.
You are receiving this email because you an Aristocrat employee.

Figure 33: Phishing example 3

From Aristocrat News <aristocratnews@aristocrat.com>   ↩ Reply   ↩ Reply All   ▾   → Fon
Subject **Penalty Notice # 0004433**
To
Date Mon, 1 Jul 2019 12:50:20 +0000
Message ID <34c2a0898d480b97c5d2202b2.26acd9633e.20190701124947.9c103d2cf6.6e5f434c@mail99.atl281.mcsv.net>
User agent MailChimp Mailer - **CID9c103d2cf626acd9633e**
Return-Path <bounce-mc.us6_12886459.808985-siggi=gooeynet.net@mail99.atl281.mcsv.net>

Hello,

Please find attached penalty notice regarding your order # 54555 made June 21 at 9:54 am.

Regards

Figure 34: Phishing example 4

I want to mention some wonderful work that ProtonMail is doing in this area. Their web client, their Android app, and—my assumption—their iPhone app display a confirmation popup when you click on a link. This is especially helpful on a smartphone, where you cannot hover over a link to reveal what is behind it. Even on a desktop, this makes it much easier to inspect a link before you allow it to open, compared to the hover method.

Here is a screenshot of the web app confirmation box in the Firefox browser:

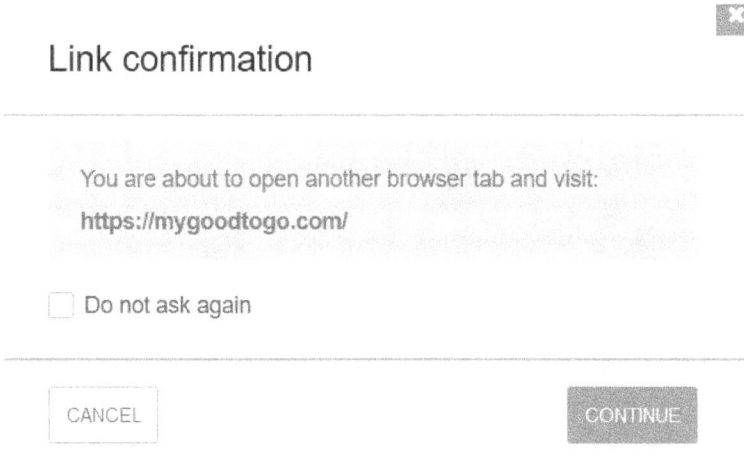

Figure 35: ProtonMail link confirmation

Common Scams

A popular scam that is making the rounds is supposedly from the Social Security Administration advising you that your SSN has been disabled due to suspicious activities. Here is a link to an article from the US Federal Trade Commission titled "Your Social Security number isn't suspended. Ever." (https://www.consumer.ftc.gov/blog/2018/09/you r-social-security-number-isnt-suspended-ever). If you need more details beyond the title, please read the blog post. Any e-mails, phone calls, or texts with this context, simply ignore them, as they are a scam.

If you get an e-mail, text, or phone call advising you that you've won a lottery or sweepstakes, you just have to prepay the taxes to collect, is a scam. Here is an excellent tweet from the Pierce County Sheriff highlighting this. Pierce County is in Washington state, with Tacoma being the largest city. Pierce County borders King County to the north. King County is the home of the biggest cities in Washington, including Seattle. (https://twitter.com/PierceSheriff/status/1124089 091300237312?s=09)

Pierce Co Sheriff
@PierceSheriff

Our fraud detectives want to warn you about a sweepstakes scam. Callers pretend to be from a mega lottery or sweepstakes & say that the taxes on the winnings need to be paid in advance in order to receive the grand prize. Please warn your elderly friends & family this is a SCAM!

Figure 36: Sweepstakes scam PCSO

If a Nigerian prince, wealthy businessman, or long-lost relative contacts you and asks you to stash their billions in your bank account for a few months in exchange for a cut of the fortune, don't do it. Best case scenario, you'll be an accomplice to money laundering, which carries a stiff federal criminal sentence in the US and most other countries. Most likely they'll clean out all of your accounts and you'll never see a dime.

Scareware

Scareware is also called extortion e-mail. This type of e-mail attempts to scare, embarrass, or shame you into paying them hush money. The e-mails follow a predictable formula. They start by talking about how you visited some site they think you might be embarrassed if anyone knew, and how, when you visited this site, malware was installed on your computer. What they are describing is something called a watering hole infection, where you get malware by visiting an untrustworthy site as I discussed in the malware section. Sometimes they claim they phished your account information, installed spyware on your computer, or installed remote access malware, and sometimes they claim they did all of it. The threat is that they used your webcam to record you on this particular website and unless you pay them hush money, they will send the proof of you accessing the site to all of your contacts that they claim their malware collected.

What they describe so far is absolutely possible, but they make other claims in their e-mails that reveal their bluff. As I have mentioned before, I'm the type of geek who has dozens of e-mail addresses; many of these are e-mail aliases. An e-mail alias is an address that is a secondary address to another account. Each e-mail account can have multiple e-mail addresses. Outlook.com, ProtonMail.com, and Gmail.com offer this feature. This way you can have an e-mail address to give out that is different from your account login. It is usually not possible to log in with anything but the primary account e-mail, so this can add a layer of security to your e-mail.

Here are some of the clues that give away the bluff of all the scareware e-mails I've seen in my inboxes.

- They all claim they hacked my account and, as proof, they claim they sent this e-mail from my hacked account. You don't need to hack an e-mail account to have that e-mail address show up in the "From" address. You just specify the name and address you want to have show up. As I discussed in the phishing section, this is easy to do.

- They also claim it is impossible for you to contact them or track them, and again, they offer as proof that they are using your account to send this e-mail. These claims fall apart in so many ways.

   o While it is easy to spoof the "From" e-mail address, it is equally easy to find out if it was spoofed. Something called the e-mail header simply tells you that it was spoofed. Most e-mail programs hide the full headers by default, for usability for inexperienced users, but they all offer a way to show them. Just perform an online search for "show full e-mail headers" (or "show source") and the e-mail provider or program you are using. When you look at the full e-mail header, you'll see all sorts of information. This includes who actually sent it, what the return path is, and more. Some of it may require experience to decode, but it is all there in plain view.

o Through viewing the headers of the sample e-mail below, I can see that this e-mail came from f719hh@furano.ne.jp. In about five minutes, I confirmed that this e-mail came from Japan, through a company called Furano Co., Ltd., in Hokkaido, Japan. Seems to be a vacation property rental company. I'm sure if I reached out to them, they could quickly tell me who f719hh is. Note that I said they could—I didn't say they would. Go back to the chapter where there is an e-mail address hosted for details of how to do this.

o When all these e-mails are addressed to e-mail aliases, you know that their hacking claim is a complete bluff.

- They also claim they have embedded an invisible image in the e-mail to tell them when you read the e-mail, and you have 48 hours to pay the hush money.

o Embedding a hidden image in an e-mail to know when the e-mail was opened is absolutely doable. In fact, I would wager that all the marketing e-

mails in your inbox are utilizing this
trick. The thing to note is that it
requires two things in order to work.

- The e-mail has to be an HTML-
  formatted e-mail; these are e-
  mails that have fancy
  formatting. If it is just a bunch
  of unformatted text, it's likely
  not HTML. You would have to
  look at the source, where the
  full headers are, to make sure.

- Your e-mail client has to
  download all embedded
  objects automatically. Those
  who care about privacy never
  have this feature turned on. I
  covered this in the privacy
  section.

- All of the scareware e-mails
  that I've seen have always been
  pure text e-mails, making
  embedding anything
  impossible.

For me personally, if anyone ever tried to give me
grief about visiting any sites, my response would
simply be, "Why is it any of your business?" Here is
an image of a sample scareware e-mail like this.

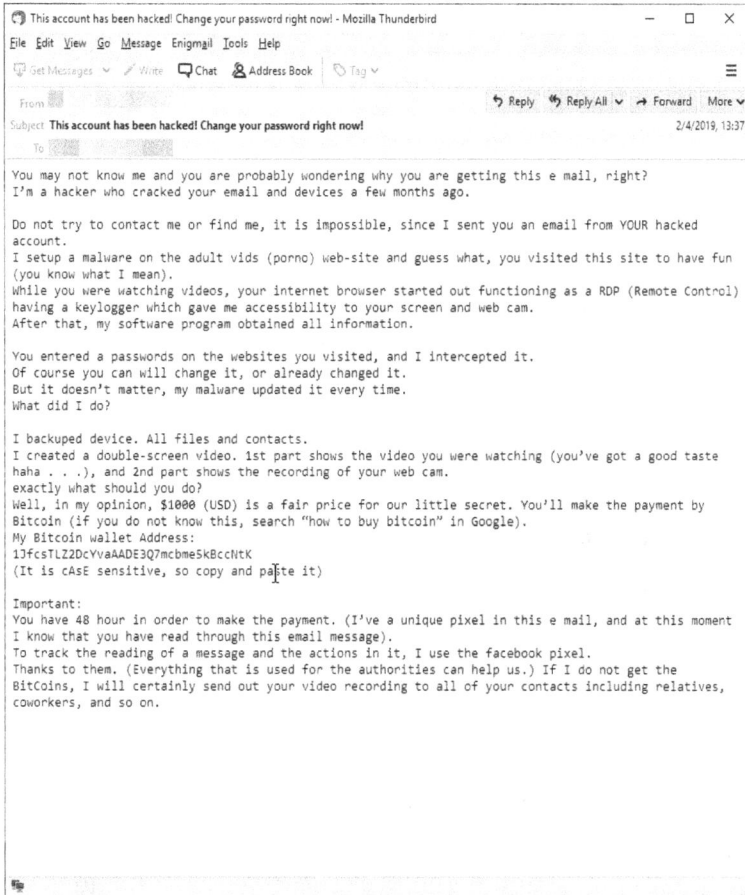

You may not know me and you are probably wondering why you are getting this e mail, right?
I'm a hacker who cracked your email and devices a few months ago.

Do not try to contact me or find me, it is impossible, since I sent you an email from YOUR hacked account.
I setup a malware on the adult vids (porno) web-site and guess what, you visited this site to have fun (you know what I mean).
While you were watching videos, your internet browser started out functioning as a RDP (Remote Control) having a keylogger which gave me accessibility to your screen and web cam.
After that, my software program obtained all information.

You entered a passwords on the websites you visited, and I intercepted it.
Of course you can will change it, or already changed it.
But it doesn't matter, my malware updated it every time.
What did I do?

I backuped device. All files and contacts.
I created a double-screen video. 1st part shows the video you were watching (you've got a good taste haha . . .), and 2nd part shows the recording of your web cam.
exactly what should you do?
Well, in my opinion, $1000 (USD) is a fair price for our little secret. You'll make the payment by Bitcoin (if you do not know this, search "how to buy bitcoin" in Google).
My Bitcoin wallet Address:
1JfcsTLZ2DcYvaAADE3Q7mcbme5kBccNtK
(It is cAsE sensitive, so copy and paste it)

Important:
You have 48 hour in order to make the payment. (I've a unique pixel in this e mail, and at this moment I know that you have read through this email message).
To track the reading of a message and the actions in it, I use the facebook pixel.
Thanks to them. (Everything that is used for the authorities can help us.) If I do not get the BitCoins, I will certainly send out your video recording to all of your contacts including relatives, coworkers, and so on.

Figure 37: Scareware sample

Fake Sales

The next scam I want to cover is something I'll call *fake sales*. The prime example of this is when I get an e-mail offering me this fabulous deal of 50 percent off this fantastic survival product that they claim is worth $90. They go on and on for pages and pages about how amazing this product is and how you must have it. They plead that if you act fast, you can have it for the fantastic price of just $45. They make claims that the MSRP was $120 and that people often find it for $90—act now and you can have it for the fantastic price of $45.

They include the full manufacturer name and model number to support their claims. For a laugh, I did some research into this amazing product. I was able to confirm that it is a well-made and respected product, but that was the only thing I was able to confirm. The manufacturer was selling that exact model on their website for $40, and Amazon was carrying it for around $25. I could not find a single place on the internet that was selling it for more than $40.

The point here is: don't trust what you read online or in your e-mail. Research and utilize your critical thinking skills. Also, notice the similarities between this scam and phishing e-mails, including the hyperbolic claims and false sense of urgency.

There is another facet to the fake sales e-mails that even well-known companies engage in, companies that you assumed were respectable. This includes pleas like "This is the last chance to save $X" events, then next week there is another urgent sale with a deadline that keeps getting extended. If something is perpetually on sale, is it really on sale? Something to ponder as homework.

Here are some screenshot examples of this.

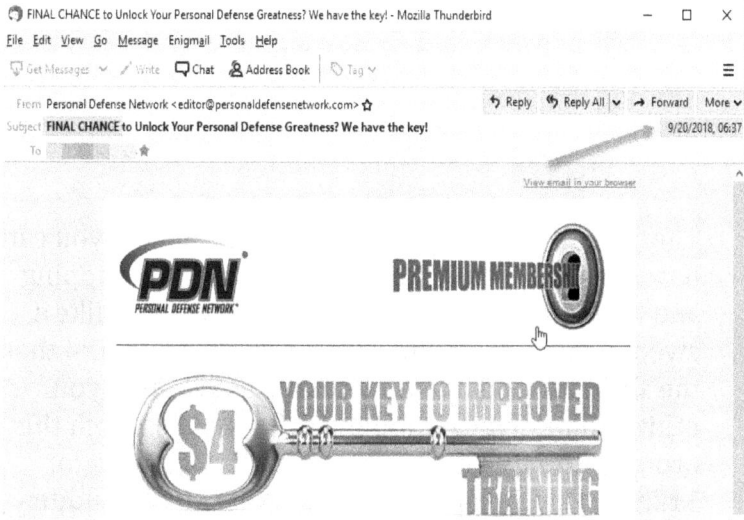

Figure 38: Final Chance sale on September 20, 2018

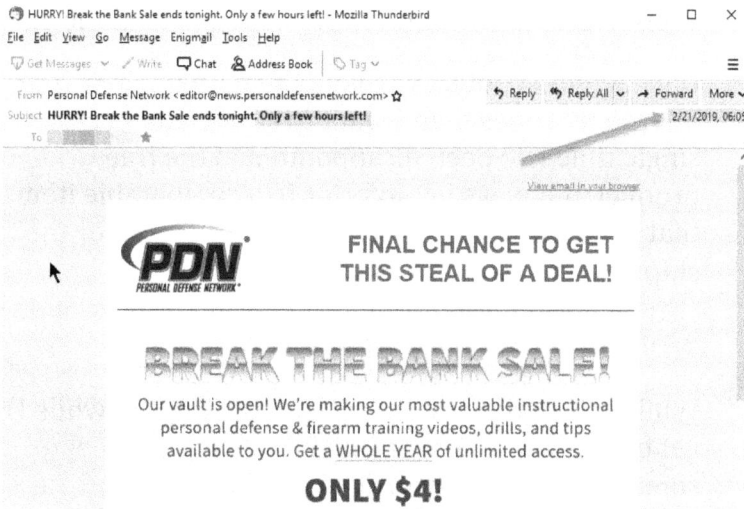

Figure 39: Same sale on February 21, 2019

As you can see, these are the same ads, just a few months apart, both attempting to claim a sense of urgency. I just confirmed that despite that ad claiming only a few hours left on February 21, 2019, on February 23, 2019 at 17:27 PST they are still offering this deal.

Free Offers

Then there are those offers that tell you how you can have this must-have item for free, just pay shipping and handling. On the surface that may sound like a sweet deal until you do a little research and find that the shipping and handling total $19.95. Then you utilize some critical thinking skills and research this product and find a comparable product online for $12.95, including free shipping. Now all of a sudden it's starting to look like a rip-off. Again, don't take anything at face value. Analyze, research, and make decisions based on actual data instead of emotions.

On a personal note, I've taken them up on their free offer more times than I want to admit, and every single time I've been disappointed in the free product. It always felt inferior to a comparable item that I bought on Amazon for less than I paid for the shipping and handling of the free item.

Saving Money on Sales

While I'm on the topic of sales, bear with me while I get on my soapbox for a bit and talk about something I'm sure you all know. If you buy something you didn't really need for 50 percent off—let's assume for the sake of argument that this was indeed 50 percent off—did you save 50 percent? Or did you waste 50 percent less money than you otherwise might have? If you legitimately had to buy something (and let's be careful about not confusing need and want here), and you found it on sale, then yes, you can say you saved money. Otherwise, you really can't. Another way to think about it: Was it already a planned purchase or did the sale ad make you want it? Spending less on a discretionary purchase is a good thing, don't get me wrong. It just bugs me when people call that saving. Anyway, I digress. Thanks for your patience while I took that little soapbox detour. I promise I'll only go on a couple more.

Bait and Switch

Alright, back to the topic at hand. The next scam I want to cover is the concept of bait and switch. This is a type of scam where they promise you one thing to bait you in, then deliver something completely different. What these scammers do to be able to claim some amount of legitimacy is they bait you with something alluring and then sell you something completely different through the use of confusing language and misdirection. They count on the fact that most people don't pay much attention to the details during the actual check-out process. Often these scammers are unnecessarily verbose, and they seem to be talking in circles. So be very cautious when purchasing from a site you don't know, and be vigilant about details. Caution and vigilance are always required; however, you need to bring that up a few notches when you are in unfamiliar territory.

Clickbait

The next topic I want to cover is the concept of clickbait. Typically, these aren't harmful, just annoying and a waste of time, although sometimes they can cause you to click onto a malware-infested site.

These start with an intriguing headline or title that sparks your interest. Maybe it makes references to the CIA or the NSA, or maybe it asks a provocative question: Are bald men more intelligent? Or they provide a partial sentence: "A survey about bald men says …" Regardless of the bait used, the objective is to get you to click on the link so that they can claim more viewers for their pointless content. Usually, what the writers are doing is writing the title in such a way that the reader is bound to jump to the conclusion they want them to, which is not actually what they meant. Kind of like what I did with the title of this book.

Congratulatory Ads

Here is another thing that may be entirely legitimate, but I find it highly annoying and unethical. One example is an e-mail that I periodically get from Citi Bank, which I generally hold in reasonably high esteem. This e-mail congratulates me for being selected to upgrade my Mastercard that I have with them and invites me to apply for an upgrade. Once I read the details, they state all sorts of benefits of having this new upgrade. Then in the fine print I find out that the annual fee for this upgraded card is $500 annually instead of the $78 annual fee on my current card, which I'm planning on canceling because I think that's too high.

Alternatively, the e-mails say something like "Congratulations! You've been selected to buy our product." These types of ad are such blatant emotional manipulation that it makes my skin crawl. I would classify these as annoying scams.

General Offer of Help

Then there are those e-mails that offer to fix your website and list all their website creation skills, yet they are vague about who they are or what website they think you need help with.

Alternatively, they offer to guarantee that your website can be found on the first page of a Google search, again with no details of which website they are talking about. Moreover, they are nowhere to be found on Google. I can only imagine what kind of ride these people would take me on if I were to respond to any of them.

The point here again is to be careful about what you read online or in your e-mail. There is so much garbage out there that it is mind-boggling. Here is great tweet from Jake Williams (@MalwareJake) where he is venting about having experienced some of this himself. Jake is a well-respected information systems security professional and the founder of Rendition Security.
(https://twitter.com/MalwareJake/status/1115956 998305193984)

Jake Williams
@MalwareJake

If you're cold emailing me pitches for SEO services, claiming you can put my company "at the top of Google's search results," why aren't you anywhere to be found when I search for you?

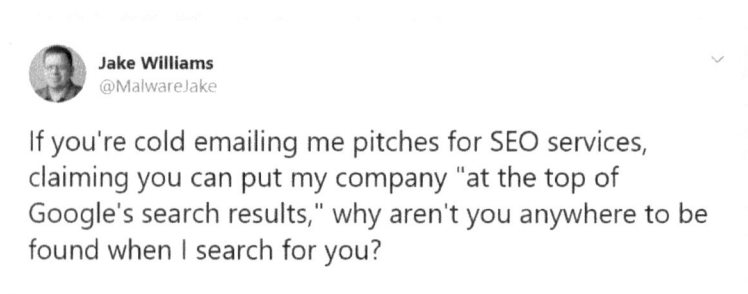

Figure 40: MalwareJake tweet

Common Themes

All of these scams, including phishing, have common themes.

- They exploit something called the fear of missing out, or FOMO. This taps into the competitive spirit of people, especially those who are into the rat race and keeping up with the Joneses. With FOMO, you are worried about being the only one who doesn't have the latest gadget or knowledge about the latest whatchamacallit.

- They try to exploit the helpful nature of others. They tend to dress it up more, but it boils down to "It would really help me out if you could give me access to your bank account so I could drain it for you."

- They are issuing a challenge. In some cases, they try to challenge you into doing something stupid. For example, the online equivalent of the drunk frat boy challenge "I bet you can't jump from this 17th-storey balcony into the swimming pool."

- Other emotional manipulations that create an urgent need to act right away, right this second, no time to think, just act—trust me, you'll thank me later.

The proper response to all of these are the same.

- Stop, think, analyze, and research.

- Don't get sucked into an emotional response.

- Never click on anything in e-mails or open attachments. Have I mentioned this one before?

In Closing

In closing, keep the following things in mind as you venture on your secure online journey.

- Don't click on stuff or open attachments in unexpected e-mails.

- Don't share your passwords. Use a unique password for every site, and never tell your passwords to anyone.

- Use a password manager to keep track of all your passwords.

- Enable MFA wherever available.

- Don't take anything online, or any other medium for that matter, at face value. Be skeptical and research everything before you believe it. A little paranoia is a good thing when it comes to being safe. Tinfoil hats are optional.

- If the content is getting you emotional, think about why that is and whether you can trust the influencers behind those reasons. Research everything to the point where you can prove it with data. Independent, critical thinking leads to increased security and a happier life.

- In my experience, unsolicited marketing mail, better known as spam, is nine times out of ten fraudulent, a scam, or a con.

- Go to
  (https://www.infosechelp.net/subscribe.php
) to sign up for email updates from us.

Appendix

References

- InfoSecHelp: https://infosechelp.net/
- ProtonMail: https://www.protonmail.com
- Traveling Mailbox: https://travelingmailbox.com/?ref=540
- 17 U.S. Code 1204. Criminal offenses and penalties. Legal Information Institute: https://www.law.cornell.edu/uscode/text/17/1204
- Private Internet Access: https://www.privateinternetaccess.com/
- Wikipedia on AOL: https://en.wikipedia.org/wiki/AOL
- Bellevue, WA Police Department on scams: https://twitter.com/BvuePD/status/1131282540994555904
- Seattle, WA Police Department on scams: https://twitter.com/SeattlePD/status/1152290701792571393
- "Netscape: The Browser that Started It All Dies a Quiet Death." *Wired* magazine: https://www.wired.com/2008/01/netscape-the-browser-that-started-it-all-dies-a-quiet-death/
- Definition of *confidentiality*: https://en.oxforddictionaries.com/definition/confidentiality
- Definition of *federation*: https://en.oxforddictionaries.com/definition/us/federation

- Definition of *integrity*:
  https://en.oxforddictionaries.com/definition/i
  ntegrity
- "The Best Hardware Security Keys for Two-
  Factor Authentication." *The Verge*:
  https://www.theverge.com/2019/2/22/18235
  173/the-best-hardware-security-keys-yubico-
  titan-key-u2f
- "Easy Ways to Build a Better P@$5w0rd."
  National Institute of Standards and Technology:
  https://www.nist.gov/blogs/taking-
  measure/easy-ways-build-better-p5w0rd
- "What business is McDonalds really in?"
  https://mpk732.wordpress.com/2015/05/16/
  what-business-is-mcdonalds-really-in/
- GSM 03.38 Wikipedia:
  https://en.wikipedia.org/wiki/GSM_03.38
- "The Secure Sockets Layer and Transport Layer
  Security." IBM:
  https://www.ibm.com/developerworks/librar
  y/ws-ssl-security/index.html
- KeePass Password Safe: https://keepass.info/
- "The Building Blocks of Good Detection and
  Response Services for the ICS Environment."
  Herlev, Denmark:
  https://ics.kaspersky.com/media/ics-
  conference-2017/Soren-Egede-Knudsen-The-
  building-blocks-of-good-detection-and-
  response-se- rvices-for-the-ICS-
  environment.pdf
- "Your Social Security Number Isn't Suspended.
  Ever." Federal Trade Commission:
  https://www.consumer.ftc.gov/blog/2018/09/

your-social-security-number-isnt-suspended-ever

- LastPass Security Report. LastPass: https://www.lastpass.com/security
- Password Strength. xkcd: https://xkcd.com/936/
- National Institute of Standards and Technology. NIST Mission, Vision, Core Competencies, and Core Values. National Institute of Standards and Technology: https://www.nist.gov/about-nist/our-organization/mission-vision-values
- 1Password: https://1password.com/
- LastPass: https://www.lastpass.com/
- Pierce County Sheriff on sweepstakes fraud: https://twitter.com/PierceSheriff/status/1124089091300237312?s=09
- Power Banks. Anker Innovations: https://www.anker.com/products/107/power-banks
- ProtonMail on Twitter: "Google Did Not Disclose Nest Secure Contained Microphones": https://twitter.com/ProtonMail/status/1098237240726208512?s=03
- DuckDuckGo Q&A on privacy: https://spreadprivacy.com/tag/duckduckgo-q-a/
- Malvertising. Center for Internet Security: https://www.cisecurity.org/blog/malvertising/
- The Caesar Cipher: http://www.cs.trincoll.edu/~crypto/historical/caesar.html

- "How Are Copyright Laws Enforced?" Legal Zoom: https://info.legalzoom.com/copyright-laws-enforced-22044.html
- Trusted. Secure. Reliable. LastPass: https://www.lastpass.com/enterprise/security
- Warriors of the Net HD. YouTube: http://www.youtube.com/watch?v=PBWhzz_Gn10
- Jake Williams on Twitter: https://twitter.com/MalwareJake/status/1115956998305193984
- "NIST's New Password Rules—What You Need to Know." Naked Security by Sophos: https://nakedsecurity.sophos.com/2016/08/18/nists-new-password-rules-what-you-need-to-know/
- Yubico. FIDO U2F. Yubico Yubi Key: https://www.yubico.com/solutions/fido-u2f/
- The Wayback Machine: https://archive.org/web/

- Dig Web Interface. Tool to decode and look up URLs: https://digwebinterface.com

www.ingramcontent.com/pod-product-compliance
Lightning Source LLC
Chambersburg PA
CBHW071228210326
41597CB00016B/1980